I0438947

Predicting Spread of Invasive Exotic Plants into Dewatered Reservoirs After Dam Removal on the Elwha River, Olympic National Park, Washington

By Andrea Woodward and Christian Torgersen, U.S. Geological Survey, and Joshua Chenoweth, Katherine Beirne, and Steve Acker, National Park Service

Open-File Report 2011-1048

U.S. Department of the Interior
U.S. Geological Survey

U.S. Department of the Interior
KEN SALAZAR, Secretary

U.S. Geological Survey
Marcia K. McNutt, Director

U.S. Geological Survey, Reston, Virginia: 2011

For more information on the USGS—the Federal source for science about the Earth, its natural and living resources, natural hazards, and the environment, visit http://www.usgs.gov or call 1-888-ASK-USGS.

For an overview of USGS information products, including maps, imagery, and publications, visit *http://www.usgs.gov/pubprod*

To order this and other USGS information products, visit *http://store.usgs.gov*

Suggested citation:
Woodward, Andrea, Torgersen, Christian, Chenoweth, Joshua, Beirne, Katherine, and Acker, Steve, 2011, Predicting spread of invasive exotic plants into de-watered reservoirs following dam removal on the Elwha River, Olympic National Park, Washington: U.S. Geological Survey Open-File Report 2011-1048, 64 p.

Contents

Figures

Tables

Conversion Factors and Datum

SI to Inch/Pound

Multiply	By	To obtain
hectare (ha)	2.471	acre
meter (m)	1.094	yard (yd)
square meter (m^2)	10.76	square foot (ft^2)
kilometer (km)	0.6214	mile (mi)
kilometer (km)	0.5400	mile, nautical (nmi)
millimeter (mm)	0.03937	inch (in.)
kilometer per hour (km/h)	0.6214	mile per hour (mi/h)
square kilometer (km^2)	247.1	acre
milligram (mg)	0.00003527	ounce, avoirdupois (oz)

Datum

Horizontal coordinate information is referenced to the North American Datum of 1983 (NAD83).

Predicting Spread of Invasive Exotic Plants into Dewatered Reservoirs After Dam Removal on the Elwha River, Olympic National Park, Washington

By Andrea Woodward and Christian Torgersen, U.S. Geological Survey, and Joshua Chenoweth, Katherine Beirne, and Steve Acker, National Park Service

Abstract

The National Park Service is planning to start the restoration of the Elwha River ecosystem in Olympic National Park by removing two high head dams beginning in 2011. The potential for dispersal of exotic plants into dewatered reservoirs following dam removal, which would inhibit restoration of native vegetation, is of great concern. We focused on predicting long-distance dispersal of invasive exotic plants rather than diffusive spread because local sources of invasive species have been surveyed. We included the long-distance dispersal vectors: wind, water, birds, beavers, ungulates, and users of roads and trails. Using information about the current distribution of invasive species from two surveys, various geographic information system techniques and models, and statistical methods, we identified high-priority areas for Park staff to treat prior to dam removal, and areas of the dewatered reservoirs at risk after dam removal.

Introduction

Background

The National Park Service (NPS) is planning the restoration of the Elwha River ecosystem in Olympic National Park by removing two high head dams beginning in 2011, which have been in place for more than 90 years. Several specific goals include restoring native anadromous fish runs and sediment transport to the coast, maintaining water quality, and re-vegetation of 276 ha of barren soil in the former reservoirs (Hoffman and Winter, 1996). These goals are inter-related such that restoring native vegetation provides necessary services to achieve the goals for fish and water quality (for example, sediment stabilization, shade). The potential for dispersal of exotic plants into dewatered reservoirs following dam removal, which would inhibit restoration of native vegetation, is of great concern (Lenhart, 2000; Shafroth and others, 2002; Zedler and Kercher, 2004; Orr and Stanley, 2006; Auble and others, 2007). Among the many potential ecological effects of invasive plants, a particular threat is the inhibition of establishment of native trees, thereby preventing shade and large woody debris inputs adequate for fish habitat (Boersma and others, 2006; Harrington and Reichard, 2007). Consequently, preventing establishment of exotic plants is the highest priority of Olympic National Park for management of the former reservoirs (Chenoweth and others, 2011). This project will (1) identify the most threatening sources of invasive plants in time for park staff to manage them, and (2) predict which areas of the former reservoirs are most at risk for exotic invasion and therefore needing the greatest focus of limited resources following dam removal.

The dam-removal project is happening in a complex jurisdictional context. The Olympic National Park boundary encompasses the upper parts of the Elwha River, the Lake Mills Reservoir, and part of the middle river section between the Elwha and Glines Canyon Dams (fig. 1). These areas comprise more than 80 percent of the drainage basin. At this time, the NPS also owns the Lake Aldwell Reservoir with eventual dispensation of the area to be determined. The land at the lower section of the river downstream of the dams is a mixture of privately owned lands, as well as lands managed by the Olympic National Forest, the Lower Elwha Klallam Tribe (LEKT), and the Washington Department of Fish and Wildlife. Parts of the estuary and nearshore are managed by Clallam County, the City of Port Angeles, and LEKT. Restoration of the drainage basin will be a multi-agency project.

Geomorphic Template for Invasion

The Elwha River flows from south to north, emptying into the Strait of Juan de Fuca (fig. 1). The Elwha Dam impounds Lake Aldwell at river km 7.9; the Glines Canyon Dam impounds Lake Mills at river km 13.7. This dam removal project will be the largest dam removal ever done in the United States (Gregory and others, 2002) and will expose deep layers of fine and coarse sediments to erosion. After dam removal, the former reservoirs will undergo dramatic morphologic and biologic succession. The free-flowing river is expected to carve a channel through the lakebed sediments leaving terraces and floodplains on its edges and removing 15–35 percent of the coarse sediments and 50 percent of the fine sediments (U.S. Department of Interior, 1996). The expected landforms will include upland slopes in one-half of the exposed area and terrace/riparian areas in the other one-half of the exposed area. The resultant spatial pattern of sediment deposition will reflect current distribution of fine sediments in deep and/or tranquil water and coarse sediments in shallow water and around points of land or any place experiencing wave action (Keddy, 1985).

Invasion Dynamics

Early efforts to predict the invasive ability of organisms focused on traits of the invader and of the community being invaded (Myers and Bazely, 2003). Invasion dynamics generally have been modeled as diffusion events (Hastings and others, 2005) using various mathematical approaches [for example, reaction-diffusion models (Buchan and Padilla, 1999), and integrodifference equations (Kot and others, 1996)]. More recently, invasion has been recognized as having two phases of dispersal. Specifically, *diffusive* dispersal occurs near the parent plant, usually zero to a few tens of meters for all plant life forms (Howe and Smallwood, 1982). In contrast, *long-distance* dispersal is a result of unusual stochastic events that move plant propagules over long distances, creating new foci for *diffusive* dispersal (Myers and Bazely, 2003). Long-distance dispersal can be defined as a minimum distance (for example, 100 m as used by Cain and others, 2000) or as some portion of the tail of a dispersal curve. Because there are few datasets to describe dispersal curves, we define long-distance dispersal as being greater than 100 m.

The reservoirs present a particular set of conditions for plant invasion. Specifically, characteristics of existing plant communities are not relevant because they do not exist, although competition with propagules of native plants will occur after the water is gone. Additionally, long-distance dispersal is of greater concern than diffusion because management staff would like to remove new foci before they begin to diffuse. Predicting the most likely sites for foci will increase the probability that foci will be located while they are still small.

Objectives

Management staff of Olympic National Park requires three basic types of information in order to minimize the effect of exotic plant invasion that might hamper efforts to restore native vegetation in the former reservoirs of the Elwha River:

1. Identification of source areas to concentrate exotic control efforts before dam removal based on current distribution of exotics and flow of vectors.
2. Identification of vulnerable sites to concentrate exotic plant control in reservoirs after dam removal.
3. Reservoirs will be accessible only by foot during 16 months of dam removal during which native and exotic seed rain, and dispersal by foot-travelers, will be driving re-vegetation. Park management needs predictions of vulnerable locations to treat and possibly plant with native plants during dam removal.

Park management will use this information (1) to prioritize areas for treatment by the Exotic Plant Management Team, and (2) to plan for effective planting of the former reservoirs. Meeting these needs constitutes the objectives of this project. Although this project addresses a specific circumstance, it also illustrates a methodology that can be applied to exotic plant datasets held by other land- management units to address other particular information needs.

Methods

Surveys of Invasive Species

The current distribution of invasive species was determined by surveys done in 2001 (Olson and others, 2001) and 2008 (as part of this project). The 2001 survey was done by foot and boat, as appropriate. Areas surveyed included the immediate shoreline (that is, within 3–10 m) of reservoirs; reservoir deltas; the river corridor between the reservoirs to at least 50 m from water's edge; the western side of the Elwha River to Herrick Road; roads within the park boundary; West Elwha, West Lake Mills and Wolf Creek Trails; the power line corridor from the Glines Canyon Dam powerhouse to the park boundary; and administrative areas, such as the ranger station, campgrounds, stock corrals, etc. (fig. 2). Occurrences of 26 target species (table 1, Survey 2001 column) were mapped using GPS or topographic maps. These species were selected using professional judgment based on species known to occur in the Elwha drainage, species listed by the Washington State Noxious Weed Board, the ability of species to invade undisturbed vegetation or riparian areas, and the difficulty of control. Population occurrence was mapped by marking the center of the population or a nearby location (if surveying from a boat). The population size was recorded in four categories: (1) 1–10 plants, (2) 11–100 plants, (3) 101–1,000 plants, or (4) greater than 1,000 plants. Extensive populations were marked with a GPS waypoint every 50–100 m, and only federal land was surveyed.

The 2001 survey was augmented in 2008 by a survey of Geyser Valley, the road north of the park boundary to U.S. Highway 101, the Hot Springs Road upstream of Glines Canyon Dam, and near Elwha Dam. Trails intersecting these areas were surveyed to 610 m elevation. This survey also was done on foot or by boat and included 4 species in addition to the 26 target species (table 1). In addition to location and population size, several environmental variables also were noted—distance to water, woody cover, habitation category (herbaceous, forest, shrubland, and lawn), the three most abundant associated species, and area infested. A total of 2,297 point locations were documented in the 588.2 ha searched across both surveys.

Spatial distribution of invasive species is displayed using kernel density maps. These maps use a color ramp to describe the density of points within cells. They are a refinement of histograms or frequency plots based on a non-parametric estimation of a probability density function and often are easier to visually interpret than a plot of individual points.

Identification of Focal Species

We identified seven *focal* taxa for detailed analysis—Canada thistle (*Cirsium arvense*), Scot's broom (*Cytisus scoparius*), herb Robert (*Geranium robertianum*), common St. John's wort (*Hypericum perforatum*), everlasting pea (*Lathyrus sylvestris*), reed canary grass (*Phalaris arundinacea*), and blackberry [*Rubus* spp.] (including Himalayan blackberry [*Rubus armeniacus*] and evergreen blackberry [*Rubus laciniatus*], table 1). We selected these species because they have great potential to cause severe environmental harm and because there is already a large enough sample size in the area to support analysis. Harmful environmental effects of these species include the ability to aggressively outcompete native vegetation (King County, 2008). In addition, dense areas of shrubby species or large grasses can prevent tree establishment and inhibit wildlife (*Rubus* spp., *Cytisus scoparius*) or fish (*Phalaris arundinacea*) movement (King County, 2008). Besides spreading rapidly and attaining 50–100 percent cover over large areas (Tisch, 1992), there are some data suggesting that *Geranium robertianum* inhibits other species through allelopathy (Barndt, 2008; Jones and Reichard, 2009). *Lathyrus sylvestris* is not included on state or county weed lists as a species of concern. Nevertheless, staff of the Olympic National Park have observed *Lathyrus sylvestris* to be extremely aggressive in the Elwha River valley, especially on riparian shorelines. Moreover, *Lathyrus sylvestris* appears to be recovering in areas where it was controlled, and it is among the most abundant exotic species (table 1).

Another group (butterfly bush [*Buddleja davidii*], English ivy [*Hedera helix*], English holly [*Ilex aquifolia*], Japanese knotweed [*Polygonum cuspidatum*], giant knotweed [*Polygonum sachalinense*], and Bohemian knotweed [*Polygonum* x *bohemicum*]) are of **high concern** because of their potential harm, but are too rare for analysis and will be removed whenever they are found (table 1). *Buddleja davidii* is of concern because it is highly invasive in riparian areas and can impede forest regeneration (King County, 2008). When *Hedera helix* covers slopes, it can contribute to slope failure by channeling water, and when it covers tree trunks, it can contribute to tree mortality as a result of windthrow or by enabling disease and rot (King County, 2008). *Ilex aquifolia* can form dense thickets and outcompete native shrubs. The *Polygonum* species can clog waterways, increase bank erosion, and impair habitat for fish and wildlife (King County, 2008).

Three other common invasive species were not considered because they are too ubiquitous to treat (orchard grass [*Dactylis glomerata*]) or are not perennial (common burdock [*Arctium minus*], bull thistle [*Cirsium vulgare*]).

Relations between Species and Environment

Environmental variables including site characteristics and distance to dispersal-vector pathways were used to predict the distribution of invasive species. Areas with invasive species were distinguished from those without by dividing the survey area into square grid cells (50×50 m). Environmental conditions and distance to dispersal-vector pathways was compared between cells with and without an invasive species. We used multiple logistic regression (Statgraphics Centurion XVI, version 16.0.08) to determine the probability of a cell having an invasive species, an approach that predicts presence or absence rather than population size (Hosmer and Lemeshow, 1989).

Explanatory variables included GIS layers describing slope, aspect, elevation, precipitation (Daymet model, University of Montana, 2010, *www.daymet.org*; Thornton and others, 1997), heat load, solar radiation in June and January, distance to water, roads and trails, and height of vegetation. Vegetation height was determined from light detection and ranging (LiDAR) elevation data by subtracting the elevation of the last return (ground level) from the first return (top of vegetation). LiDAR data were collected in April 2009 (Entrix, 2009). We grouped the heights into classes to describe physiognomic groups—bare (0 m), herbaceous (0–0.33 m), low shrubs (0.33–1.67 m), tall shrubs (1.67–3.33 m), deciduous trees and young conifers (3.33–13.33 m), and conifers (> 13.33 m). Grid cells were described by the percentage of LiDAR cells (1 m^2) in each height category.

Analyses were done for focal species (table 2) over the entire study area and by subareas. Subareas are meant to reflect regions with similar exposure to invasive species vectors and similar habitat. These areas include Lake Aldwell, Lake Aldwell Delta, the area between U.S. Highway 101 and Glines Canyon Dam plus the Wolf Creek Trail, Lake Mills, Lake Mills Delta, Geyser Valley and Hot Springs Road (fig. 3). The area labeled Hot Springs Road was not analyzed because results would not describe an environment relevant to conditions expected in the dewatered reservoirs.

Additionally, logistic regression was used to determine the probability of occurrence of (1) any focal exotic species, or (2) any exotic species surveyed (table 1) for the subarea from Glines Canyon Dam to U.S. Highway 101. This subarea is affected by all long-distance dispersal vectors and is physically similar to what is expected for the dewatered reservoirs. These equations were used to calculate the probability of invasive plant occurrence in 50×50 m grid cells drawn over the dewatered reservoirs using current lake bathymetry to describe slope, aspect, and to estimate where the river course will form.

Invasive Communities

Multiple invasive species were present at many survey sites. We used cluster analysis of survey sites having any surveyed species (table 1) that occurred in at least 5 percent of the sites to look for associations among invasive species. These species included *Acrtium minus, Cirsium arvensis, Cirsium vulgare, Cytisus scoparius, Dactylis glomerata, Geranium robertianum, Hypericum perforatum, Lathyrus sylvestris, Phalaris arundinacea, Rubu*s spp., curley dock (*Rumex crispus*), and peavine (*Vicia* spp.). The analysis used rank Bray-Curtis resemblances among sites for species abundance codes (PRIMER-E version 6, Clarke and Gorley, 2006) to assign plots to hierarchically nested groups. To see how these clusters corresponded to groups identified by the non-metric multidimensional scaling (MDS) ordination technique and geographic regions, we mapped clusters having rank 100,000 onto the ordination, and geographically in the Elwha River valley. The level 100,000 was selected to represent a desirable amount of discrimination among groups after examination of the dendrogram. Non-metric multi-dimensional scaling is a non-parametric ordination technique that is useful for discerning patterns in plant community structure relative to environmental gradients because it is robust to common violations of statistical assumptions required by other ordination techniques (Minchin, 1987). Non-metric multi-dimensional scaling maximizes the rank-order correlation between distance measures (Bray-Curtis resemblance in this case) and distance in ordination space (represented as a two- or three-dimensional graph), with "stress" as a measure of the mismatch between these distances (Clarke and Warwick, 2001). Stress values less than 0.1 indicate a reliably interpretable ordination; ordinations with stress values from 0.1 to 0.2 are less reliable, especially at the high end of the range, and conclusions should be cross-checked against alternative analyses such as cluster analysis (Clarke and Warwick, 2001).

Wind Dispersal

Frequency of wind speed and direction during seed dispersal (July 15–September 30) were determined using 10 years of weather data from the Remote Automated Weather Stations (RAWS) site near Hurricane Ridge Visitors Center. Potential destinations and sources for wind-dispersed species were predicted using the wind model WindNinja (Forthofer, 2007; Forthofer and others, 2009). The model uses an approach based on fluid dynamics to model wind speed and direction at 6 m above vegetation height derived from a digital elevation model in a geographic information system (GIS). We used a 200-m grid cell resolution and modeled wind speed and direction expected throughout the study area if it were measured from the north, east, and south at Hurricane Ridge at the maximum wind speed from each direction over the 10 years of data (that is, north, 15 m/s; east, 12 m/s; south, 18 m/s). Wind from the west was not modeled because it occurs infrequently during July through September.

The accuracy of WindNinja model results for the three directions and wind speeds were evaluated by comparing the prediction for the Glines Canyon Dam with actual wind speeds measured at the dam. Wind speed and direction at Glines Canyon Dam were measured by an anemometer established February 12, 2009, which reports 15 min averages. We identified periods during the anemometer record when conditions at Hurricane Ridge (averaged over 10 min) were within 5 degrees and 1 m/s of the three modeled conditions. Then actual conditions at Glines Canyon Dam during these periods were compared with model predictions from the four points estimated by WindNinja that were closest to the dam.

Long-Distance Dispersal Mechanisms of Focal Species

Cirsium arvense

Cirsium arvense seeds have a pappus loosely attached to the achene. When the pappus remains attached to the seed, it has excellent aerodynamics (Sheldon and Burrows, 1973) and is capable of traveling several kilometers (Wood and del Moral, 2000). In a controlled experiment, Sheldon and Burrows (1973) reported a maximum seed dispersal of 11.35 m in wind speeds of 16.41 km/h. The minimum dispersal in low wind speeds (5.47 km/h) was 3.79 m. Meadow thistle (*Cirsium dissectum*) seeds with a slightly higher falling velocity have been observed to travel up to 1 km with winds up to 4.3 m/s (Soons and others, 2004) and 22.7 percent of seeds traveled more than 100 m when horizontal wind speed was 1.5 m/s with updrafts and the terrain was descending (Tackenberg, 2003). However, the pappus readily separates from the achene, which will prevent effective long-distance seed dispersal (Bostock and Benton, 1979; Jacobs and others, 2006). Water transport of seeds and plant fragments also is an effective means of dispersal (Washington State, 2009), and seeds have periods of 36.5 and 54.5 h until 50 and 90 percent of seeds sink , respectively (Boedeltje and others, 2003). Seeds are dispersed mid-summer through autumn and a patch of Canada thistle (a single plant) is capable of producing as many as 250,000 seeds (Boersma and others, 2006).

Cytisus scoparius

Regionally, *Cytisus scoparius* is spread by humans (Neubert and Parker, 2004). Locally, the primary mode of seed dispersal for *Cytisus scoparius* occurs when the seed pods ripen and ballistically launch the seed from the parent plant (Zouhar, 2005; Boersma and others, 2006). In one study, the average dispersal distance was 2.34 m with a maximum distance of 7.25 m; greater than 10 percent of the seeds traveled more than 5 m, whereas just less than 5 percent did not leave the pods (Malo, 2004). In another study, seeds dispersed 10 m from a Scot's broom thicket, although the mode of dispersal was unclear (Zouhar, 2005). Ants, other animals, and flowing water (hydrochory) are known to disperse Scot's broom seed (King County, 2008). However, although *Cytisus scoparius* seeds will float, it is only for a few hours, and vegetative propagation from transported plant pieces has not been observed in nature (Watterson and Jones, 2006). Nevertheless, floods and debris flows have been implicated in transporting *Cytisus scoparius* from roads to streambeds and then farther downstream at sites in western Oregon (Watterson and Jones, 2006). Seeds are dispersed in the summer and possibly into early autumn as seedpods dry. Seeds can persist for many years in soil (Zouhar, 2005). A single shrub is capable of producing thousands of seeds in 1 year (Zouhar, 2005) but 80 percent of plants do not flower until 4 years of age (Sheppard and others, 2002).

Geranium robertianum

The seeds are forcibly ejected from the plant up to 6.5 m away (Tofts, 2004). Seeds are further dispersed by animals and machinery. Specifically, a sticky fiber at one end of the seed attaches readily to vegetation or animals (Boersma and others, 2006), providing an opportunity for long-distance dispersal. This form of dispersal is not specific for animal species. The sticky seeds frequently disperse on hikers' shoes along trail corridors and along roads by cars, mowers, and weed-eaters. Although *Geranium robertianum* has not been described as experiencing hydrochory by some sources (Tofts, 2004; King County, 2008) and was not collected from the water near terrestrial populations (Goodson and others, 2003), hydrochory may be a minor mechanism of dispersal (Grime and others, 1988; Goodson and others, 2003; Tofts, 2004). Herb Robert seeds can remain viable in the soil for up to 5 years, but germination rates decreased significantly after the first year (Tofts, 2004). In Europe, plants typically produced 100–300 seeds (Tofts, 2004) and may flower more than once in a calendar year.

Hypericum perforatum

Hypericum perforatum primarily propagates by seed (Boersma and others, 2006). Although the small sticky seeds have no specific adaptations for wind dispersal, Tisdale and others (1959) found that seeds readily traveled 3, 6, and 9.1 m downwind of parent plants, although most of the seeds fell in the 3-m zone, and seeds have a relatively low falling velocity (Tackenberg, 2001). However, the primary mode of long-distance dispersal is likely to be zoochorous; the seeds are borne in sticky capsules that readily adhere indiscriminately to the bodies of birds and mammals (Zouhar, 2005). In the Elwha River valley, *Hypericum perforatum* populations are predominantly found on riparian landforms. Plants are capable of producing seed in the first year after germination and individual plants can produce from 15,000 to 23,350 seeds (Tisdale and others, 1959), which disperse from late summer into autumn.

Lathyrus sylvestris

The major reproductive strategy of *Lathyrus sylvestris* appears to be by rhizomes, but when seeds are produced, the primary dispersal mechanism appears to be ballistic. The seedpods twist and eject the seeds upon maturation (Godt and Hamrick, 1991). Although seeds are dispersed between 1 and 20 m from the parent plants of perennial pea (*Lathyrus latifolius*), dispersal is not as far for *Lathyrus sylvestris* because of shorter pods and the position of the seeds in the pods (Hossaert and Valero, 1988).

Phalaris arundinacea

Phalaris arundinacea primarily propagates vegetatively, but is capable of prolific seed production—up to 600 seeds per stem (Tu and others, 2004). However, germination and seedling establishment rates are low (Stannard and Crawder, 2001; Tu and others, 2004). Indeterminate maturation of seeds, which generally occurs in summer, prolongs the season of dispersal (Stannard and Crawder, 2001). *Phalaris arundinacea* seeds are small, dense, and naked (Stannard and Crawder, 2001), with no specific adaptations for wind or other dispersal mechanism (NatureServe, 2008). Nevertheless, seeds can be wind dispersed (Rhoads and Block, 2002). Seeds also can float for a few days and then germinate on drained soil (Piper, 1924; Coops and Van der Velde, 1995). Shoots also can arise from the nodes of water-dispersed culms (Marten and Heath, 1973).

Rubus armeniacus and Rubus lacinatus

The fleshy fruit is a food source for birds and mammals, including non-native species of rats and birds, such as European starlings (*Sturnus vulgaris*) (Boersma and others, 2006). Because the fruits are highly desirable, they do not remain on the plant for very long (Tirmenstein, 1989). Seeds are dispersed late summer through early autumn.

Distribution of Invasives

Spatial Distribution

Invasive species are densely distributed in the Elwha River valley near the river, in the reservoir deltas, and along roads (fig. 4). The area south of U.S. Highway 101 and west of the Elwha River was not surveyed because the land is privately owned.

Locations of 30 invasive species were documented in 2,297 records (table 1). Among these site records, the focal species *Cirsium arvense*, *Geranium robertianum*, *Phalaris arundinacea,* and *Lathyrus sylvestris* were the most common (table 2). Other common species included *Dactylis glomerata* (348 records), *Cirsium vulgare* (361 records), and *Arctium minus* (136 records) (table 1). The focal species *Hypericum perforatum*, *Cytisus scoparius*, and *Rubus* spp. were less abundant (table 2). The areas with the highest frequency of observations of invasive species include the Lake Aldwell Delta and the area between Glines Canyon Dam and U.S. Highway 101 (table 2).

Distributions of seven focal species indicate that the species are all present between Glines Canyon Dam and U.S. Highway 101 (fig. 5). The greatest concentration of *Cirsium arvense* is in Geyser Valley (including Humes Ranch), upstream of roads. Likely vectors to this area could be wind, pack stock, other animals, or hikers. Elsewhere, *Cirsium arvense* is distributed along roads and in the reservoir deltas and appears to be spreading locally from sites of long-distance dispersal. *Cytisus scoparius* is found near the dams and in the Elwha River valley in a pattern that suggests human introduction followed by hydrologic spread. *Geranium robertianum* also occurs in Geyser Valley mostly associated with the Elwha River and Lake Aldwell Delta. A high concentration of *Geranium robertianum* is near the base of the trail that leads to private land to the west of the Elwha River and may be heavily used by elk (see fig. 4). The pattern suggests possible introduction by animals, vehicles, or machinery followed by hydrologic spread, or spread by anglers from infested campgrounds to fishing spots along the river. *Hypericum perforatum* has a similar pattern to *Geranium robertianum*, but is more closely associated with roads. *Lathyrus sylvestris* and *Phalaris arundinacea* occur along the river between Glines Canyon Dam and Lake Aldwell Delta with distribution patterns that suggest hydrologic spread. *Rubus* spp. is found along the road and near the base of the trail to Herrick Road.

In general, the distribution patterns of invasive species in the Elwha River valley suggest that long-distance dispersal to the area primarily was by humans and possibly wind and animals. Once present, patterns of invasive species distribution are consistent with spread by local diffusion (vegetatively and by short distance seed dispersal) and by the river. Spread along the river may be hydrologic or may be a result of animals and people that travel along the river corridor.

Factors Predicting Species Distribution

Environmental variables and vector proximity (defined in next paragraph) explained the occurrence of invasive species but the relative importance of each differed among species and locations (table 3). Interpretation of logistic regression results are complicated by a number of factors. First, not all potential sites are filled. Consequently, the model describes where species tend to first establish rather than where they are capable of invading. Moreover, the number of infested cells is small compared with the total number of cells analyzed (see table 2 and fig. 2 for numbers by area and species). Thus, the models are better at predicting uninfested cells than infested cells. Furthermore, a grid cell size of 50 m is quite large compared with the scale of microsite characteristics that likely are affecting the establishment success of invasive species. This analysis is designed to clarify the broad-scale environmental factors affecting the patterns that are visually discernible in the distribution maps (fig. 5).

Results are presented as odds ratios where a value of 1.0 indicates that the variable has no predictive ability; values greater than 1.0 indicate a higher probability of species occurrence in association with the variable; values less than 1.0 indicate a lower probability of occurrence in association with the variable. For vector proximity, however, the variable is distance from the features (that is, road, trail, water). Consequently, values less than 1.0 indicate a low probability of occurrence with greater distance from the feature, which is a positive association with the feature. Odds ratios for these models are very close to 1.0, indicating that none of the vector proximity variables has a high predictive ability. This is partially a result of the many cells adjacent to roads that do not have exotic species even though the species may only occur close to roads. Odds ratios are most useful for indicating the relative importance of variables in the logistic model.

Among the long-distance dispersal vectors, water dispersal (hydrochory) was expected to be important for *Phalaris arundinacea*, but also appears to be important for predicting occurrence of all species except *Rubus* spp. and *Hypericum perforatum*. The predictive ability of the road was important for all species in the area between Glines Canyon Dam and U.S. Highway 101, except for *Phalaris arundinacea* (that is, the primary water-dispersed species) and important overall for *Cytisus scoparius*, *Lathyrus sylvestris*, and *Rubus* spp. Trails are significant predictors only for *Lathyrus sylvestis* and *Rubus* spp., with odds ratios very close to 1.0.

Among environmental variables, elevation was inversely associated with invasive species occurrence (table 3). This reflects the greater abundance of invasive species in the valley bottom and downriver. Elevation was not predictive overall for *Cirsium arvense* and *Geranium robertianum*, which are distributed throughout the study area. Elevation is associated with *Hypericum perforatum*, which also occurs from Geyser Valley to Elwha Dam. Slope, aspect, heat load, and solar radiation were not good predictors of invasive species occurrence, and precipitation had inconsistent relationships. However, vegetation did have relatively high predictive ability. Specifically, bare ground was negatively associated with invasive species occurrence, whereas herbs, low shrubs, and low trees were positively associated with invasive species. The associations with bare ground (negative) and herbs (positive) may simply indicate the presence of the invasive species. The positive association with low shrubs and low trees (presumably deciduous) may indicate a protective environment that traps seeds but does not create too much shade. Although *Geranium robertianum* is shade tolerant (Tofts, 2004), it does not seem to have a stronger association with tall vegetation than other species, with the exception of a strong association with tall shrubs at Lake Aldwell Delta (odds ratio of 1.177 is the second strongest site-specific association).

In the subarea between Glines Canyon Dam and U.S. Highway 101, the probability of occurrence of any invasive plant species or any focal invasive plant species was related to proximity to roads, elevation, low shrubs, and low trees (table 3). Occurrence of all invasive species also was predicted by herbs; all focal invasives were predicted by precipitation, slope, and solar radiation in July.

Associations among Invasive Species

Most groups identified by the cluster analysis (fig. 6) had only one species or were dominated by that species. These groups tended to occupy different regions of the ordination (fig. 7), validating that these groups are distinct entities.

Because the groups of sites identified by cluster analysis and ordination largely indicate the presence of only one species, the map of groups (fig. 8) is similar to the maps of individual species (fig. 5). Geographically, sites dominated by *Cirsium arvense* (group f) are found at Lake Mills Delta and Geyser Valley (fig. 8). *Geranium robertianum*-dominated communities (group k) primarily are in Geyser Valley, the deltas, and associated with roads. The groups associated with *Dactylis glomerata* and *Phalaris arundinacea* (groups j and l) are found near the lakes and the river. The least differentiated group (group m) has representatives throughout the survey area.

Wind Vector

The importance of predominantly wind-dispersed species to populate barren areas was documented following the eruption of Mount St. Helens (that is, 34 seeds/0.1 m^2/yr of mostly wind-dispersed species; Wood and del Moral, 2000). In the Elwha River valley, *Cirsium arvense* is the only one of the seven focal taxa that has seeds or fruits that are adapted for wind dispersal. *Hypericum perforatum* primarily is dispersed by animals but seeds have a relatively low falling velocity (Tackenberg, 2001). *Polygonum* spp., which is a species of concern but not a focal species for analysis, propagates primarily by vegetative means, but has fruits that are morphologically adapted to aid air transport for long-distance dispersal (Beerling and others, 1994; Zhou and others, 2003).

Mechanistic models have been developed to predict the long-distance dispersal of seeds by wind (Greene and Johnson, 1989; Okubo and Levin, 1989; Nathan and others, 2001; Tackenberg, 2003). These models are based on modeling the trajectory of seeds as a function of the falling velocity imparted by seed morphology and wind dynamics. Some of these models can be made spatially explicit because they have the ability to incorporate terrain. However, these models are quite complex and are computationally expensive. Moreover, many of the models are only effective at predicting short-distance transport (Tackenberg, 2003). As these models have advanced, several lessons have been learned regarding factors affecting long-distance transport:

- Uplifting of seeds and fruits is necessary for long-distance dispersal (Tackenberg, Poschlod, and Kahmen, 2003), especially for low-growing species (Tackenberg, Poschold, and Bonn, 2003). In forests, updrafts are created by high horizontal wind velocity creating turbulence (Horn and others, 2001; Nathan and others, 2002). In grasslands, high winds also are important (Soons and others, 2004), but a more prominent process is high surface heating in the presence of low horizontal wind velocity, which can result in convective uplift (Tackenberg, 2003).

- In addition to high winds, seed release height, height of surrounding vegetation, and seed or fruit falling velocity determine dispersal distance (Soons and others, 2004).
- Species with falling velocity less than 1.5 m/s have a high potential for long-distance dispersal (Tackenberg, 2003). Falling velocity of several invasive species present in the Elwha River valley or related species (table 4) confirm that *Cirsium arvense* is the most likely focal species to be wind dispersed followed by *Hypericum perforatum*.
- Topography and forest gaps can create mechanical turbulence, which can affect seed or fruit distribution. Specifically, downdrafts forming at the upwind edge of gaps can deposit propagules whereas updrafts at the downwind edge can lead to long-distance transport (Nathan and others, 2005).
- Topography that descends in the direction of airflow can enhance dispersal of species with falling velocities greater than 0.25 m/s, but those with falling velocities of 1.6 m/s are too heavy for topography to matter (Tackenberg, 2003).
- Strong vertical winds common in thunderstorms may lift even heavy seeds or fruits (Higgins and others, 2001).

Wind Direction and Speed during Seed Dispersal

All three potentially wind dispersed species produce seed from mid-summer through early autumn. During this time (July 15–September 30), winds averaged over a 10-yr period are primarily from the north to north-northeast, east and south-southeast to south-southwest with a maximum speed of 18 m/s (table 5). Although wind speeds in at least the 9–12 m/s range were recorded from nearly all directions, and up to 15–18 m/s from the south, winds were typically less than 6 m/s (fig. 9). These values are based on the average of wind measurements taken for 10 min at hourly intervals, consequently higher gusts may have occurred.

Effect of Topography on Wind Direction

We validated the WindNinja model by comparing actual wind speed at Glines Canyon Dam with the model predictions based on wind speed measured at Hurricane Ridge. Results show that incidences of the same conditions at Hurricane Ridge can result in a wide range of conditions at Glines Canyon Dam (table 6). On average, the actual conditions at Glines Canyon Dam match fairly well with predictions for easterly and southerly winds at Hurricane Ridge. The complex topography of Glines Canyon to the north of the dam, including the dam itself and adjacent berm, may create turbulence that reduces the comparability of wind speed and direction measured at the dam with the WindNinja predictions. In fact, southerly readings at the anemometer have been observed during northerly prevailing winds (Roger Hoffman, Olympic National Park, oral commun., 2010)

Output from WindNinja shows how the speed and direction of wind flowing primarily from the north, south, and east at Hurricane Ridge will be altered by the mountainous topography of the Elwha River valley (figs. 10–12). Areas upwind of the reservoirs are potential sources of exotic species as indicated in black. However, it is likely that seeds will be dropped in areas of light wind. Consequently, areas where the wind reaches the reservoirs without decreasing to less than 11 m/s are considered high priority areas to treat before and after dam removal and are marked in green.

Winds from the east and south are most likely to disperse *Cirsium arvense* from current concentrations to the dewatered reservoirs (table 7). If these populations cannot be eradicated before dam removal and access can be obtained during dam removal, then removal of any seed heads that protrude above the rest of the vegetation will decrease seed production and dispersal (Soons and others,

2004). This approach also can be used with any remaining *Polygonum* spp. populations to prevent rare wind dispersal events.

The wind model output also identifies several areas that could be sources of invasive species but do not have recorded surveys (table 8). These are areas to target for eradication efforts prior to dam removal.

Spatial heterogeneity of vegetation height can create patterns of wind turbulence that may affect plant dispersal (Nathan and others, 2005), such that air currents associated with forest gaps may pull wind-dispersed seeds from surrounding areas (Wenny, 2001). Specifically, uplift eddies can be produced between the center of a 250-m forest gap and the upwind forest edge, and downdrafts can occur at the downwind edge of the gap, potentially leading to disproportionate deposition of seeds. LiDAR-based images of the reservoirs show that tall vegetation forms a fairly abrupt edge around the Lake Mills Reservoir (fig. 13). Patterns of vegetation height are much more complex around the Lake Aldwell Reservoir, reflecting the higher diversity of land uses. The effects of patterns of vegetation height on airflow are not addressed in the WindNinja model.

Water Vector

The expectation that *Phalaris arundinacea* primarily is a water-dispersed species is supported by logistic regression results (odds ratios <1, indicating positive association in table 3). Studies of propagules trapped from rivers indicate that vegetative diaspores outnumber seeds (Boedeltje and others, 2003, 2004). However, seeds are well adapted to hydrochory with 50 percent of a test group of seeds sinking after 19.9 or 41.0 h (T_{50}) and 90 percent after 38.3 (Coops and van der Velde, 1995) or 71.5 h (Boedeltje and others, 2003).

Cytisus scoparius, *Lathyrus sylvestris*, *Geranium robertianum*, and *Cirsium arvense* may be carried by the river but also are associated with roads (fig. 14 and table 3). *Cytisus scoparius* may be transported in debris flows (Watterson and Jones, 2006) that may result from dam removal activities. *Geranium robertianum* may have some potential for hydrochory (Goodson and others, 2003) and *Lathyrus sylvestris* propagates primarily vegetatively, so it seems likely that pieces could be effectively moved by water. *Cirsium arvense* generally is found along the road and in fields and openings, but also is associated with the river (fig. 13) and can potentially be transported by water. Seeds of *Cirsium arvense* will float (Boedeltje and others, 2003) and transport of plant fragments also is effective (Washington State, 2009). Other factors, such as people and animals that travel the river corridor, cannot be dismissed as potential vectors creating these patterns, although animals are not considered to be effective long-distance dispersers of at least *Cytisus scoparius* (Bossard, 1991).

Making spatial predictions about the distribution of plant propagules resulting from hydrochory is hampered by not knowing the future course of the river through the dewatered reservoirs. However, we propose that certain areas should be carefully searched as the river develops a path. Based on release of seeds into an artificial flume (Merritt and Wohl, 2002) and rhizomes of water buttercup (*Ranunculus lingua*) into a river in Sweden (Johansson and Nilsson, 1993), several conclusions about likely sites of propagule deposition can be drawn. First, more propagules are deposited in areas of slow flow (for example, eddies, flow expansions, point bars, pool margins, slackwaters, near obstacles and in curved river stretches) than in areas of faster flow (for example, cut banks, flow constrictions, islands, straight margins). Second, propagules will be left at high water levels, and then will be left in bands that reflect temporary stations of the water's edge as the hydrograph declines.

Before dam removal, high-priority areas for species removal should include drainages that currently flow into the lakes from east and west in addition to removing potentially hydrochorous species upriver. No exotic species were captured flowing into Lake Mills and only one was captured flowing out in a recent trapping survey (Brown and Chenoweth, 2008). Additionally, *Cytisus scoparius* and *Polygonum* spp. have the potential to be moved in mudslides and other earth movement that originate from dam removal activities at Glines Canyon Dam. Records exist for *Cytisus scoparius* at the dam (fig. 5) and for *Polygonum* spp. on the road leading to the dam.

Mammal Vectors

Geranium robertianum and *Hypericum perforatum* are the two focal species with adaptations that facilitate dispersal by animals. However, other species may attach to (epizoochory) or be ingested by (endozoochory) herbivores, either intentionally or inadvertently. For example, Carey's smartweed (*Polygonum careyi*) and *Rubus* spp. have been observed to germinate from feces of white-tailed deer (*Odocoileus virginianus*) in the eastern United States (Myers and others, 2004). However, the *Polygonum* species of concern in the Elwha River valley typically are much taller than *Polygonum careyi*, placing seeds mostly out of the reach of deer.

Patterns of movement of several elk (*Cervus elaphus roosevelti*) herds are available for the Elwha River valley (figs. 15 and 16). The herd that frequents the Herrick Road area (fig. 15) does not travel to Lake Mills, nor does it cross U.S. Highway 101 to Lake Aldwell. This pattern may persist following dam removal if elk are not inclined to pass through Glines Canyon. This herd warrants observation, however, because they have the potential to disperse the many invasive species occurring in the river valley between Glines Canyon and U.S. Highway 101 as well as the potential to disperse species occurring in the Herrick Road area on private land not surveyed. The herd near Lake Mills (fig. 16) was observed near Dodger Point in summer, Geyser Valley in spring and autumn, and near Lake Mills from December to February. All points along the Whiskey Bend Road were recorded during January and February (Patti Happe, Olympic National Park, oral commun., 2010). A second collared elk from this herd showed a similar pattern but did not go near the lake during the milder winter of 2009–10. The greatest danger of invasive spread associated with these elk is the potential to transfer species from Geyser Valley to the dewatered Lake Mills Reservoir when the elk move downriver from autumn to winter during harsh winters. If seeds are still present on invasive species occurring on the eastern side of Lake Mills in the Whiskey Bend area, they also could be transported to Lake Mills by elk during winter.

Black-tailed deer (*Odocoileus hemionus*) also are present in the Elwha River valley, but detailed information regarding distribution and movements is available only for the area between Whiskey Bend and the Lillian River (Jenkins and others, 1999). These animals were more abundant on south- and southwest-facing slopes adjoining bottomlands on slopes less than 20 degrees. They preferentially frequented alder flats and old fields but also spent considerable time in coniferous forests. Home ranges averaged 51 ha and individuals moved 85–470 m daily. Density was estimated at 4.64–6.58 deer/km^2 for the whole area depending on the estimation method; density was estimated at 11.1 deer/km^2 for the northern side of the river where favorable exposures occur. Several animals left the area in May and June and migrated south to higher elevations, returning by the end of October. If these numbers are consistent for the rest of the area affected by dam removal, then deer have a substantial potential to spread invasive species to all habitats.

Beavers (*Castor canadensis*) are active on the Elwha River, but sign primarily is limited to cut stems of shrubs and trees, rather than structures (Knapp, 2009). Sign is most abundant downstream of the Elwha Dam but also occurs on the western side of Lake Aldwell, between U.S. Highway 101 and

Glines Canyon and on both reservoir deltas (fig. 17). These beavers are bank dwellers and prefer willow species. However, there are records of beaver cutting *Cytisus scoparius* (Knapp, 2009) and *Polygonum* spp. (Cathy Lucero, Clallam County, oral commun., 2009). The greatest potential for long-distance dispersal comes from den failure as a result of flooding or other disturbance, which would distribute the den contents downstream. Because beavers tend to stay close to water for protection from predators and need food and construction resources to be nearby, beavers will not likely establish dens in the dewatered reservoirs until after they are vegetated. However, if the new river course should establish close to extant or planted willow, cottonwood, or alder stands, then beaver may be attracted.

Bird Vectors

Rubus spp. is the only taxon among the focal taxa adapted for endozoochory, especially by birds but also by coyotes (*Canis latrans*), foxes (*Vulpes fulva*), squirrels (*Tamiasciurus douglasii*), and black bears (*Ursus amicanus*) (Hoshovsky, 2000). However, *Hedera helix* and *Ilex aquifolia* are of high concern even though they are relatively rare. *Cytisus scoparius* has been observed to be spread by grouse and quail in coastal areas of the Pacific Northwest (Bossard, 1991). Seeds of *Geranium robertianum* and *Hypericum perforatum* are adapted for attachment to birds and mammals.

Distributions of bird species in the region of the Elwha River that will be affected by dam removal have been surveyed to predict distributions after dam removal (Gelarden, 2008). Of the 42 species observed, the 4 most common species that inhabit riparian areas include the American robin (*Turdis migratorius*), chestnut-backed chickadee (*Poecile rufescens*), Swainson's thrush (*Catharus ustulatus*), and warbling vireo (*Vireo gilvus*). Of the four species, Swainson's thrush and warbling vireo have lower numbers and are migratory, leaving in August and September, and may miss seed dispersal for some invasive plant species. Based on surveys and habitat models, Gelarden (2008) estimated a high density of chestnut-backed chickadees throughout the area. The other three taxa share similar areas of high density, including Geyser Valley, Lake Mills Delta, the northeastern shore of Lake Mills, north of Glines Canyon, the area near the park boundary, and the Herrick Road area (fig. 18). These areas coincide with observations of all three bird-dispersed invasive species; hence, they constitute targets for invasive species treatment prior to dam removal.

Perhaps the most important observation relative to restoration of the Elwha reservoirs is that seeds dispersed by birds tend to cluster near plantings (Robinson and Handel, 2000). Given the infeasibility of modeling movements of tens of birds species, perhaps the most important place to look for bird-dispersed invasive species is in areas with newly established woody vegetation and in planted areas.

Road- and Trail-Associated Vectors

All focal species except *Phalaris arundinacea* are associated with roads (fig. 4, table 2), and roads may have been the initial pathway for most of the invasives in the Elwha River valley. *C. scoparius* appears to have been introduced at the maintenance yard due west of the Elwha Ranger Station and may now be dispersing down the river. *Rubus* spp. and *Lathyrus sylvestris* also are associated with trails according to logistic regression results (table 2), although visually *Geranium robertianum* has a stronger relation than *Rubus* spp. (fig. 18). To the extent that trail dispersal is a result of people and livestock, it will not be a concern during dam removal because trails will be closed. In addition, a vehicle and equipment de-contamination protocol has been developed for all construction and other vehicles that will access the area during dam removal (Chenoweth and others, 2011).

Priority Areas

In summary, the ultimate goal of this project is to identify high priority areas where invasive plants should be removed before dam removal, and to predict areas of the dewatered reservoirs that are likely to be infested before dam removal. To accomplish these goals, we analyzed several spatial datasets to identify source areas for vectors and to describe the relationships among species locations and environmental conditions, including relationships to vectors (fig. 19). The outcomes are maps showing areas and environments within those areas to treat before dam removal, and vulnerable areas in the reservoirs after dam removal.

Pre-Dam Removal Treatments

Areas that constitute sources for each individual vector of invasive plants are described in sections on vectors above. When the source areas are combined on one map (fig. 20), the area between U.S. Highway 101 and Glines Canyon Dam-Lake Mills is the potential source for the greatest number of vectors. This area also has the greatest density and diversity of invasive species (figs. 4 and 5).

Environments within these areas where invasive species are most likely to occur can be mapped based on the results of logistic regression (table 3). Specifically, the significant ($\alpha \leq 0.05$) variables are proximity to water, roads, trails and cover of bare ground, herbs, low shrubs, and low trees. Tall shrubs also are significant ($\alpha \leq 0.05$) predictors for *Geranium robertianum*. High resolution maps of the source areas (figs. 21–25) show where these conditions exist.

Transport of *Cirsium arvense* by wind is the greatest threat from the area north of Lake Aldwell. Because this area is largely privately owned, the populations of *Cirsium arvense* are significant, and the search area is extensive, the most effective way to lessen this threat may be with a public campaign to enlist support for keeping the area mowed, especially during flowering.

In the area between Lake Aldwell and the Elwha Campground, the river, and road corridors, the Herrick Road area and the hillslope to the south are potential sources of invasive plants. Because this area experiences all vectors (that is, wind, mammals, birds, roads, and trails) and there are many known locations of invasive plants, this is a significant potential source, primarily for the Lake Aldwell Reservoir. Because the Herrick Road area is privately owned, this is another place where encouraging mowing could be an effective strategy for minimizing the sources for exotic plants. However, mowing must be timed when *Geranium robertianum* is not in seed and mower blades should be high enough to avoid picking up *Geranium robertianum* seeds.

Between Elwha Campground and Lake Mills, the green areas associated with the river, roads, and trails are most likely to have invasive species. Many of these areas already have been searched and populations mapped, but perhaps more attention should be paid to the areas between the roads just north of the lake, and between the road and the lake on the western side of the lake, especially for bird-dispersed species.

Large populations of invasive plants have been mapped on the delta at the southern end of Lake Mills and the lake edge. Other high priority areas are the slope and drainages on western edge of the southern part of the lake.

Geyser Valley has many instances of *Cirsium arvense*, *Geranium robertianum*, and *Hypericum perforatum*. *Cirsium arvense* is abundant, and although it is not likely to spread to the reservoirs by wind, it may be carried by water. Consequently, all three species should be considered threats.

Setting Priorities for Treatments and Species

It will not be possible to treat all areas and invasive plant species before dam removal. Consequently, it is necessary to establish priorities. Priorities for species can be set be considering the vector for each, whether each species is likely to use the expected habitat, and the consequences of establishment in terms of time to produce seeds, difficulty of removal, and rate of spread once established (table 9). Regarding vectors, it can be argued that water is the most important because of its proximity, followed by wind because of potential distances affected. Elk currently are not very active near Lake Aldwell and elk near Lake Mills are mostly frequenting the interior of the park. Birds likely will not be important until trees have been planted. Regarding factors other than vectors, species that are quick to produce seed, are adapted to the environment, are difficult to remove, and spread quickly should have the highest priority for removal. Species with all these characteristics among the priority group already identified include *Buddleja* spp., *Cirsium arvense*, *Phalaris arundinacea,* and *Polygonum* spp. (table 9).

Priority areas for treatment can be identified from those described in section, "Pre-Dam Removal Treatment" by considering whether priority areas are inside or outside of the park, which vectors are active, and how many species are known to be present (table 10). For areas that have not been searched outside of the park, advocating mowing is appropriate for the Herrick Road area and north of Lake Aldwell.

For areas that have been searched and are inside the park, the area between the reservoirs is known to have the highest density and diversity of invasive species. Given the size of the area, however, it may be best to focus on the known sites of the priority species. The areas around the dams also will experience significant disturbance and should be cleaned of exotics before dam removal begins. Finally, the deltas also are known hot spots of invasive species and especially should be cleared of those species that are spread by water.

For areas that are inside the park but have not been searched, the highest priority is the appropriate environments (fig. 24) within the plateau and drainages on the west side of the south end of Lake Mills. This area has many active vectors and the potential to have several high priority species in close proximity to the dewatered reservoir.

Species Locations Outside of Olympic National Park

Few geo-referenced data describing locations of exotic species have been collected by others outside of Olympic National Park. However, some records are available for locations of species that have been treated for invasive species on Olympic National Forest lands north of Olympic National Park (fig. 26). These records give some indication of what can be expected outside of the park. An additional source of invasive plants is the commercial gravel pit owned by Shaw and Lane, located just off of Olympic Hot Springs Road. This pit is a source of *Polygonum* spp. and *Cytisus scoparius* at least (Cathy Lucero, Clallam County, oral commun., 2009).

Post-Dam Removal Vulnerability

Predicting areas of the dewatered reservoirs vulnerable to invasive species is hampered by a number of challenges. First, we do not know where the river course will establish and hence the location of an important dispersal vector. Second, we do not know what form the topography of the reservoirs will take. Finally, even if we had a detailed prediction of future reservoir conditions, we do not have high-resolution descriptions of site preference for invasive plants. Nevertheless, we can use current reservoir bathymetry and predictive equations from logistic regression to make some crude forecasts (figs. 27 and 28). Results vary somewhat depending on whether the predictions are based on occurrences of all invasive species or only on the focal species, with higher resolution coming from the focal species-based predictions. These predictions are based on the distribution of invasive plants between Glines Canyon Dam and U.S. Highway 101; the efficacy of this approach to show that pattern is shown in figure 29.

Several stochastic factors that can only be observed during and after dam removal and that affect the vulnerability of areas to invasive plants are not captured in these maps:
- Areas of slack water because of obstructions (for example, large woody debris), bends in river course, etc. can be observed only after the new river course develops.
- The importance of short-distance dispersal and vicinity to current infestation of invasive plants is not incorporated.
- The effects of vegetation, especially trees, on wind deposition are not included but likely will result in deposition on the western edge of Lake Aldwell and the eastern edge of Lake Mills during easterly winds.
- There is a greater chance of aerial long-distance dispersal during thunderstorms.
- Elk are more likely to move to lower elevations where they have greater opportunity to spread invasive plants during cold, snowy winters than during mild winters.

Additionally, areas newly planted with trees and shrubs as part of revegetation efforts are especially vulnerable to bird- and worker-dispersed invasive species.

Conclusions

Protecting the dewatered reservoirs from invasive species is an important part of restoring native vegetation; we have used observational data, knowledge of species biology, and various statistical analyses and models to focus these efforts. Specifically, we have selected species locations from multiple surveys and integrated them with environmental data and distribution of vectors using GIS to identify priority areas and environments within those areas for treatment of or search for invasive species. High priority areas to treat inside of the Olympic National Park include (1) the dam sites, (2) the area between the lakes, and (3) the deltas. The high priority area to search for invasives that has not been searched is the plateau and drainages on the western side of the southern end of Lake Mills. High priority areas to search and treat should access be granted include (1) the Herrick Road area, (2) areas due north of Lake Aldwell, (3) the gravel pit near Olympic Hot Springs Road, and (4) the hillslope east of Lake Aldwell. Next, we used information regarding the high priority species to further prioritize to which species the limited resources for treatment should be applied. High priority species include *Cirsum arvense*, *Buddleja* spp., *Phalaris arundinacea*, and *Polygonum* spp. Finally, we used the current relationships between species distribution and environment to predict where species may establish in the reservoirs based on current bathymetry. Predicting what will happen in the reservoirs after dam removal is extremely speculative because we cannot predict where the new river channel will form. In this case, the most productive way to address invasive spread is to recognize that water is likely the most important vector soon after dam removal and that areas of slack water are the most likely places where invasive species will establish.

Acknowledgments

We are grateful to the field crew members who conducted the two surveys for invasive species: Mignonne Bivin, Phillip Blackcrow, Garth Hopie, Wendy McClure, Caitlin McNulty, Kathleen Mitchell, and Tolle Murphy. Roger Hoffman participated in discussions leading to the development of the project and helped interpret data from the anemometer at Glines Canyon Dam. Cathy Lucero provided information about Clallam County weed records. Laurie Kurth provided us with example output from WindNinja. Susan Piper provided digital records of invasive species found on Forest Service lands. We also would like to thank Tracy Fuentes, Diane Doss, and one anonymous reviewer for their thoughtful and thorough reviews of this report.

References Cited

Auble, G.T., Shafroth, P.B., Scott, M.L., and Roelle, J.E., 2007, Early vegetation development on an exposed reservoir: implications for dam removal: Environmental Management, v. 39, p. 806–818.

Barndt, J.K., 2008, An assessment of allelopathic potential of herb Robert (*Geranium robertianum*): Seattle, Wash., University of Washington, M.S. thesis.

Beerling, D.J., Bailey, J.P., and Conolly, A.P., 1994, Biological flora of the British Isles—*Fallopia japonica* (Houtt.) Ronse Decraene (*Reynoutria japonica* Houtt., *Polygonum cuspidatum* Sieb. & Zucc.): Journal of Ecology, v. 82, no. 4, p. 959–979.

Boedeltje, G., Bakker, J.P., Bekker, R.M., van Groenendael, J.M., and Soesbergen, M., 2003, Plant dispersal in a lowland stream in relation to occurrence and three specific life-history traits of the species in the species pool: Journal of Ecology, v. 91, p. 855–866.

Boedeltje, G., Bakker, J.P., Ten Brinke, A., van Groenendael, J.M., and Soesbergen, M., 2004, Dispersal phenology of hydrochorous plants in relation to discharge, seed release time and buoyancy of seeds: the flood pulse concept supported: Journal of Ecology, v. 92, no. 5, p. 786–796.

Boersma, P.D., Reichard, S.H., and VanBuren, A.N., eds., 2006, Invasive species in the Pacific Northwest: Seattle, Washington, University of Washington Press.

Bossard, C.C., 1991, The role of habitat disturbance, seed predation and ant dispersal on establishment of the exotic shrub *Cytisus scoparius* in California: American Midland Naturalist, v. 126, p. 1–13.

Bostock, S.J., and Benton, R.A., 1979, The reproductive strategies of five perennial compositae: Journal of Ecology, v. 67, no. 1, p. 91–107.

Brown, R.L., and Chenoweth, J., 2008, The effect of Glines Canyon Dam on hydrochorous seed dispersal in the Elwha River: Northwest Science, v. 82 (special issue), p. 197–209.

Buchan, L.A.J., and Padilla, D.K., 1999, Estimating the probability of long-distance overland dispersal of invading aquatic species: Ecological Applications, v. 9, p. 254–265.

Cain, M.L., Milligan, B.G., and Strand, A.E., 2000, Long-distance seed dispersal in plant populations: American Journal of Botany, v. 87, p. 1217–1227.

Chenoweth, J., Acker, S., and McHenry, M.L., 2011, Revegetation and restoration plan for Lake Mills and Lake Aldwell: National Park Service and Lower Klallam Tribe, http://www.nps.gov/olym/naturescience/Elwha-Restoration-Plans.htm.

Clarke, K.R, and Gorley, R.N., 2006, PRIMER v6: User Manual/Tutorial: Plymouth, U.K., PRIMER-E Ltd.

Clarke, K.R., and Warwick, R.M., 2001, Change in marine communities—an approach to statistical analysis and interpretation (2d ed.): Plymouth, U.K., PRIMER-E Ltd.

Coops, H., and van der Velde, 1995, Seed dispersal, germination and seedling growth of six helophyte species in relation to water level zonation: Freshwater Biology, v. 34, p. 13–20.

Entrix, 2009, LiDAR Survey of Lower Elwha River, Clallam County, Washington. Entrix, Inc., Seattle, Washington.

Forthofer, J.M., 2007, Modeling wind in complex terrain for use in fire spread prediction: Fort Collins, Colorado, Colorado State University, M.S. thesis.

Forthofer, J.M., Shannon, K., and Butler, B., 2009, Simulation diurnally driven slope winds with WindNinja: Proceedings of 8th Symposium on Fire and Forest Meteorological Society, Kalispell, Montana, October 13–15, 2009.

Gelarden, C.J., 2008, Forecasting avian response to Elwha River restoration: Bellingham, Washington, Western Washington University, M.S. thesis.

Godt, M.J.W., and Hamrick, J.L., 1991, Genetic variation in *Lathyrus latifolius* (Leguminosae): American Journal of Botany, v. 78, p. 1163–1171.

Goodson, J.M., Gurnell, A.M., Angold, P.G., and Morrissey, I.P., 2003, Evidence for hydrochory and the deposition of viable seeds within winter flow-deposited sediments: the river Dove, Derbyshire, U.K.: River Research and Applications, v. 19, p. 317–334.

Greene, D.F., and Johnson, E.A., 1989, A model of wind dispersal of winged or plumed seeds: Ecology, v. 70, p. 339–347.

Gregory, S., Li, H., and Li, J., 2002, The conceptual basis for ecological responses to dam removal: BioScience, v. 52, p. 713–723.

Grime, J.P., Hodgson, J.G., and Hunt, R., 1988, Comparative Plant Ecology: A Functional Approach to Common British Species: London, Unwin Hyman.

Harrington, T.B., and Reichard, S.H., 2007, Meeting the challenge: invasive plants in Pacific Northwest ecosystems: USDA Forest Service General Technical Report PNW-GTR-694.

Hastings, A., Cuddington, K., Davies, K.F., Dugaw, C.J., Elmnedorf, S., Freestone, Amy, Harrison, Susan, Holland, Matthew, Lambrinos, John, Malvadkar, Urmila, Melbourne, B.A., Morre, Kara, Taylor, Caz, Thomson, Diane, 2005, The spatial spread of invasions—New developments in theory and evidence: Ecology Letters, v. 8, issue 1, p. 91–101, doi:10.1111/j.1461-0248.2004.00687.x.

Higgins, S.I., Richardson, D.M., and Cowling, R.M., 2001, Validation of a spatial simulation model of a spreading alien plant population: Journal of Applied Ecology, v. 38, p. 123–132.

Hoffman, C.H., and Winter, B.D., 1996, Restoring aquatic environments—a case study of the Elwha River, *in* Wright, R.G., ed., National Parks and Protected Areas—Their Role in Environmental Protection: Cambridge, Mass., Blackwell Scientific, p. 303–323.

Horn, H.S., Nathan, R.A.N., and Kaplan, S.R., 2001, Long-distance dispersal of tree seeds by wind: Ecological Research, v. 16, p. 877–885.

Hoshovsky, M.C., 2000, Rubus discolor, *in* Bossard, J.M., Randall, J.M., and Hoshovsky, M.C., eds., Invasive Plants of California's Wildlands: Berkeley, California, University of California Press, p. 277–281.

Hosmer, D.W., and Lemeshow, S., 1989, Applied Logistic Regression: New York, John Wiley and Sons.

Hossaert, M., and Valero, M., 1988, Effect of ovule position in the pod on patterns of seed formation in two species of *Lathyrus* (Leguminosae: Papilionoidas): American Journal of Botany, v. 75, p. 1714–1731.

Howe, H.F., and Smallwood, J., 1982, Ecology of seed dispersal: Annual Review of Ecology and Systematics, v. 13, p. 201–228.

Jacobs, J., Sciegienka, J., and Menalled, F., 2006, Ecology and management of Canada thistle [Cirsium arvense (L.) Scop.]: Washington, D.C., U.S. Department of Agriculture, Natural Resource Conservation Service Invasive Species Technical Note No. MT-5.

Jenkins, K.J., Happe, P.J., Hoffman, R., Beirne, K., and Fieberg, J., 1999, Wolf prey base studies in Olympic National Park, Washington—final report: U.S. Geological Survey Forest and Rangeland Ecosystem Science Center, Olympic Field Station FWS Agreement No. 1448-13410-98-N007, p. 66.

Johansson, M.E., and Nilsson, C., 1993, Hydrochory, population dynamics and distribution of the clonal aquatic plant *Ranunculus lingua*: Journal of Ecology, v. 81, p. 81–91.

Jones, C.C., and Reichard, S., 2009, Current and potential distributions of three non-native plants in the contiguous U.S.A.: Natural Areas Journal, v. 29, p. 332–343.

Keddy. P.A., 1985, Quantifying a within-lake gradient of wave energy in Gillifillan Lake, Nova Scotia: Canadian Journal of Botany, v. 62, p. 301–309.

King County, 2008, Best Management Practices and Regulatory Guidelines, *in* Noxious Weeds, King County, Washington: King County website, accessed October 19, 2009, at *http://kingcounty.gov/weeds*.

Knapp, R.L., 2009, Northern American beaver *Castor canadensis* habitat use in the Olympic Peninsula's Elwha Valley: Bellingham, Washington, Western Washington University, M.S. thesis.

Kot, M., Lewis, M., and van den Driessche, P., 1996, Dispersal data and the spread of invading organisms: Ecology, v. 77, p. 2027–2042.

Lenhart, C.F., 2000, The vegetation and hydrology of impoundments after dam removal in southern Wisconsin: Madison, Wisconsin, University of Wisconsin, M.S. thesis.

Malo, J.E., 2004, Potential ballistic dispersal of *Cytisus scoparius* (Fabaceae) seeds: Australian Journal of Botany, v. 52, p. 653–658.

Marten, G.C., and Heath, M.E., 1973, Reed canarygrass, *in* Heath, M.E., Metcalfe, D.S., and Barnes, R.F., eds., Forages—The science of grassland agriculture: Ames, Iowa, The Iowa State University Press.

Merritt, D.M., and Wohl, E.E., 2002, Processes governing hydrochory along rivers—hydraulics, hydrology, and dispersal phenology: Ecological Applications, v. 12, p. 1071–1087.

Minchin, P.R., 1987, An evaluation of the relative robustness of techniques for ecological ordination: Vegetation, v. 69, p. 89–107.

Myers, J.A., Bellend, M., Gardescu, S., and Marks, P.L., 2004, Seed dispersal by white-tailed deer—implications for long-distance dispersal, invasion, and migration of plants in eastern North America: Oecologia, v. 139, p. 35–44.

Myers, J.H., and Bazely, D.R., 2003, Ecology and Control of Introduced Plants: New York, Cambridge University Press.

Nathan, R., Katul, G.G., Horn, H.S, Thomas, S.M., Oren, R., Avissar, R., Pacala, S.W., and Levin, S.A., 2002, Mechanisms of long-distance dispersal of seed by wind: Nature, v. 418, p. 409–413.

Nathan, R., Safriel, U.N., and Noy-Meir, I., 2001, Field validation and sensitivity analysis of a mechanistic model for tree seed dispersal by wind: Ecology, v. 82, p. 374–388.

Nathan, R., Sapir, N., Trakhtenbrot, A., Katul, G.G., Bohrer, G., Otte, M., Avissar, R., Soons, M.B., Horn, H.S., Wikelski, M., and Levin, S.A., 2005, Long-distance biological transport processes through the air—can nature's complexity be unfolded *in silico?*: Diversity and Distributions, v. 11, p. 131–137.

NatureServe, 2008, NatureServe Explorer—An online encyclopedia of life: NatureServe website, accessed December 16, 2008, at *http://www.natureserve.org/explorer*.

Neubert, M.G., and Parker, I.M., 2004, Projecting rates of spread for invasive species: Risk Analysis, v. 24, p. 817–831.

Okubo, A., and Levin, S.A., 1989, A theoretical framework for data analysis of wind dispersal by wind: Ecology, v. 82, p.374–388.

Olson, R.W., Mitchell, K.E., and Murphy, T.B, 2001, Survey of selected non-native plants within the Elwha River ecosystem restoration project area, Port Angeles, Washington, Olympic National Park.

Orr, C.H., and Stanley, E.H., 2006, Vegetation development and restoration potential of drained reservoirs following dam removal in Wisconsin: River Research and Applications, v. 22, p. 281–295.

Piper, C.V., 1924, Forage plants and their culture, Revised edition: New York, MacMillan.

Rhoads, A.F., and Block, T.A., 2002, Reed canarygrass (*Phalaris arundinacea* L.): Philadelphia, Pa., Morris Arboretum of the University of Pennsylvania website, accessed December 16, 2008, at: *http://www.paflora.org/Phalaris%20arundinacea.pdf.*

Robinson, G.R., and Handel, S.N., 2000, Directing spatial patterns of recruitment during an experimental urban woodland reclamation: Ecological Applications, v. 10, p. 174–188.

Shafroth, P.B., Friedman, J.M., Auble, G.T., Scott, M.L., and Braatne, J.H., 2002, Potential responses of riparian vegetation to dam removal: BioScience, v. 52, p. 703–712.

Sheldon, J.C., and Burrows, F.M., 1973, The dispersal effectiveness of the achene-pappus units of selected compositae in steady winds with convection: New Phytologist, v. 72, p. 665–675.

Sheppard, A.W., Hodge, P., Paynter, Q., and Rees, M., 2002, Factors affecting invasion and persistence of broom *Cytisus scoparius* in Australia: Journal of Applied Ecology, v. 39, no. 4, p. 721–734.

Soons, M.B, Gerrit, W.H., Nathan, R., and Katul, G.G., 2004, Determinants of long-distance seed dispersal by wind in grasslands: Ecology, v. 85, p. 3056–3068.

Stannard, M., and Crawder, W., 2001, Technical Note 43—Biology, history, and suppression of reed canarygrass (*Phalaris arundinacea* L.), *in* Technical notes, U.S. Department of Agriculture, Natural Resources Conservation Service, Publications—Pullman Plant Materials Center website, accessed December 16, 2008, at *http://plant-materials.nrcs.usda.gov/wapmc/publications.html.*

Tackenberg, O., 2001, Methoden zur Bewertung gradueller Unterschiede des Ausbreitungspotentials von Pflanzenarten, Modellierung des Windausbreitungspotentials und regelbasierte Ableitung des Fernausbreitungspotentials: Marburg, Germany, Ph.D dissertation (Also available at http://archiv.ub.uni-marburg.de/diss/z2001/0107).

Tackenberg, O., 2003, Modeling long-distance dispersal of plant diaspores by wind: Ecological Monographs, v. 73, p.173–189.

Tackenberg, O., Poschlod, P., and Bonn, S., 2003, Assessment of wind dispersal potential in plant species: Ecological Monographs, v. 73, p. 191–205.

Tackenberg, O., Poschlod, P., and Kahmen, S., 2003, Dandelion seed dispersal—the horizontal wind does not matter for long-distance dispersal—it is updraft!: Plant Biology, v. 5, p. 451–454.

Thornton, P.E., Running, S.W., and White, M.A., 1997, Generating surfaces of daily meteorological variables over large regions of complex terrain: Journal of Hydrology, v. 190, p. 214–251.

Tirmensteina, D., 1989, *Rubus discolor, in* Fire Effects Information System: Washington, D.C., U.S. Department of Agriculture, Forest Service, Rocky Mountain Research Station, Fire Sciences Laboratory website, accessed November 24, 2008, at *http://www.fs.fed.us/database/feis/.*

Tisch, E., 1992, Alien weed threatens Olympic National Park—Voice of the Wild Olympics: Newsletter of Olympic Park Associates, v. 1, p. 6.

Tisdale, E.W, Hironaka, M., and Pringle, W.L., 1959, Observations on the autecology of *Hypericum perforatum*: Ecology, v. 40, p. 54–62.

Tofts, R.J., 2004, Biological Flora of the British Isles—*Geranium robertianum* L.: Journal of Ecology, v. 92, no. 234, p. 537–555.

Tu, M., Soll, J., and Lipinski, B., 2004, Reed canarygrass (*Phalaris arundinacea*), control and management in the Pacific Northwest: Portland, Oregon, The Nature Conservancy, Oregon Field Office.

University of Montana, 2010, Daymet: Missoula, Mont., University of Montana, Numerical Terradynamic Simulation Group website, accessed December 5, 2010, at *http://www.daymet.org/*.

U.S. Department of the Interior, 1996, Sediment analysis and modeling of the river erosion alternative: Washington, D.C., Bureau of Reclamation Elwha Technical Series no. PN-95-9.

Washington State, 2009, Washington State Noxious Weed Control Board: Olympia, Wash., Washington State Noxious Weed Control website, accessed October 15, 2009, at *http://www.nwcb.wa.gov/*.

Watterson, N.A., and Jones, J.A., 2006, Flood and debris flow interactions with roads promote the invasion of exotic plants along steep mountain streams, western Oregon: Geomorphology, v. 78, p. 107–123.

Wenny, D., 2001, Advantages of seed dispersal—a re-evaluation of directed dispersal: Evolutionary Ecology Research, v. 3, p. 51–74.

Wood, J., and del Moral, R., 2000, Seed rain during primary succession on Mount St. Helens, Washington: Madrono, v. 47, p. 1–9.

Zedler, J.B., and Kercher, S., 2004, Causes and consequences of invasive plants in wetlands: opportunities, opportunists, and outcomes: Critical Reviews in Plant Sciences, v. 23, p. 431–452.

Zhou, Z., Miwa, M., Nara, K., Wu, B., Nakayg, H., Lian, C., Miyashita, N., Oishi, R., Maruta, E., and Hogetsu, T., 2003, Patch establishment and development of a clonal plant, *Polygonum cuspidatum*, on Mount Fuji: Molecular Ecology, v. 12, p. 1361–1373.

Zouhar, K., 2005, *Cytisus scoparius, C. striatus, in* Fire Effects Information System: Washington, D.C., U.S. Department of Agriculture, Forest Service, Rocky Mountain Research Station, Fire Sciences Laboratory website, accessed November 24, 2008, at *http://www.fs.fed.us/database/feis/*.

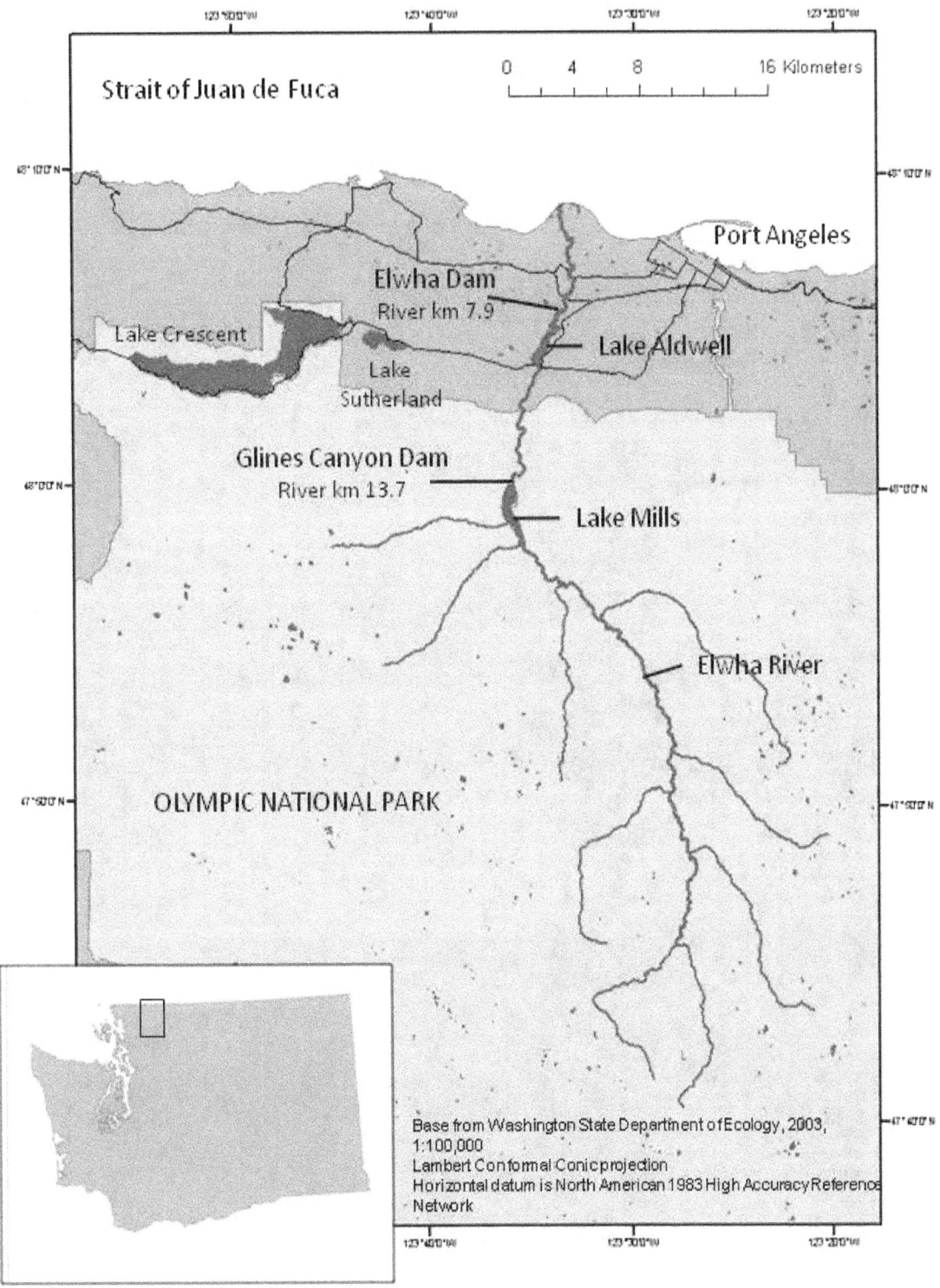

Figure 1. Locations of the Elwha and Glines Canyon Dams and respective reservoirs on the Elwha River, Olympic National Park, Washington.

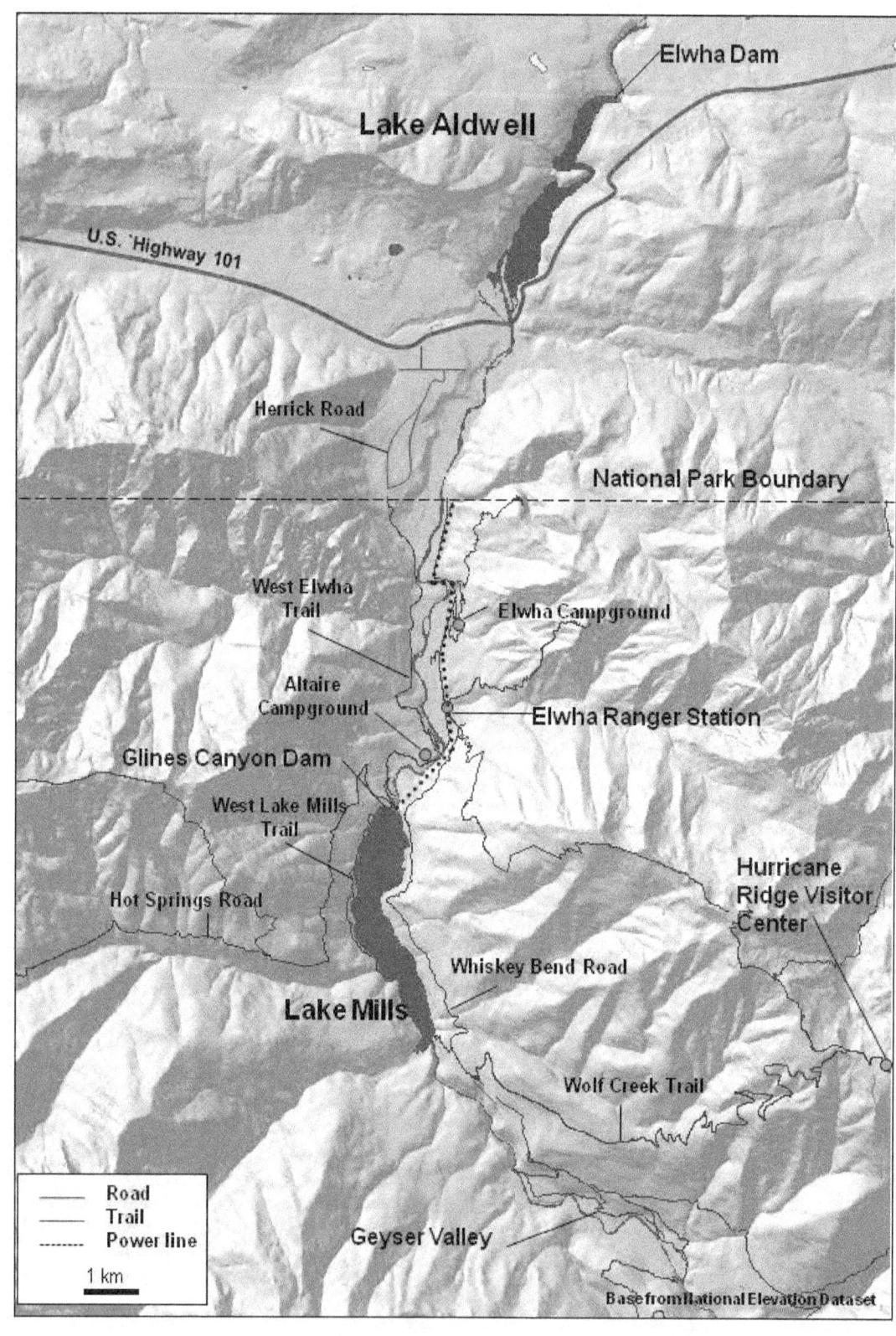

Figure 2. Project area, Elwha River, Olympic National Park, Washington.

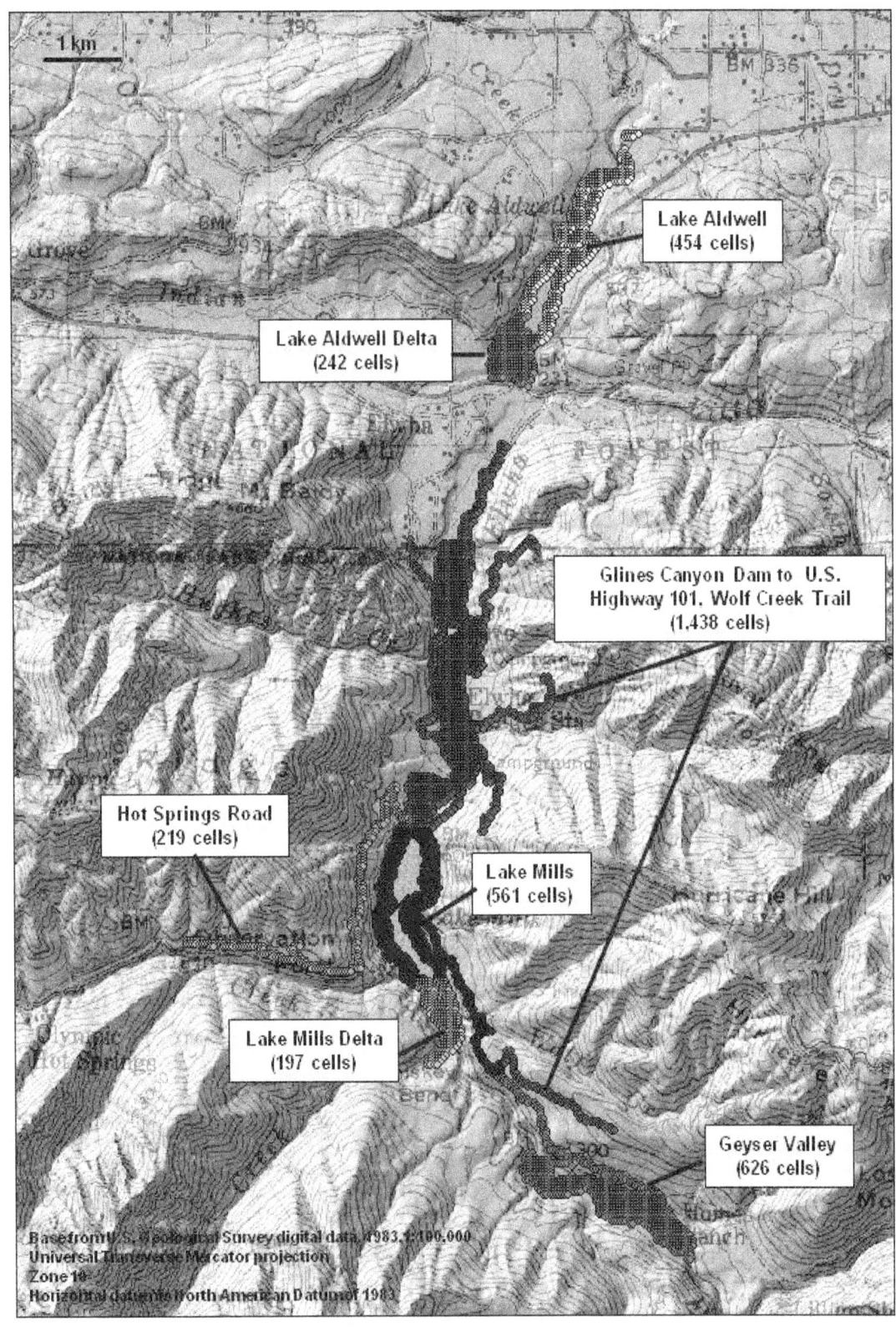

Figure 3. Subareas used to determine predictive variables for occurrence of invasive plant species, Elwha River, Olympic National Park, Washington.

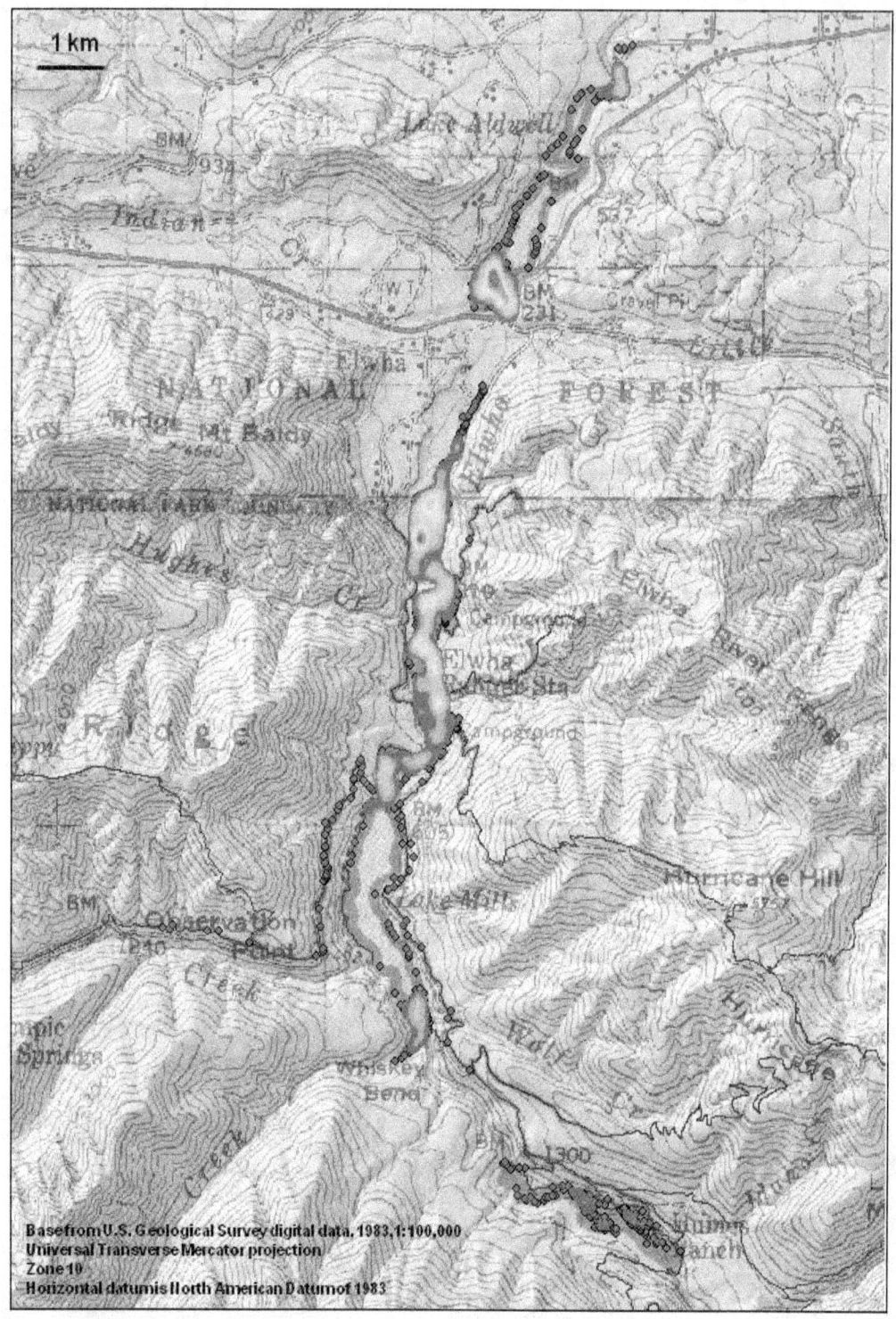

Figure 4. Kernel density representation of 'hot spots' of 30 invasive species (table 1; high to low density represented by hot to cool colors), isolated observations (green points), and area surveyed during 2001 and 2008 (lilac), Elwha River, Olympic National Park, Washington.

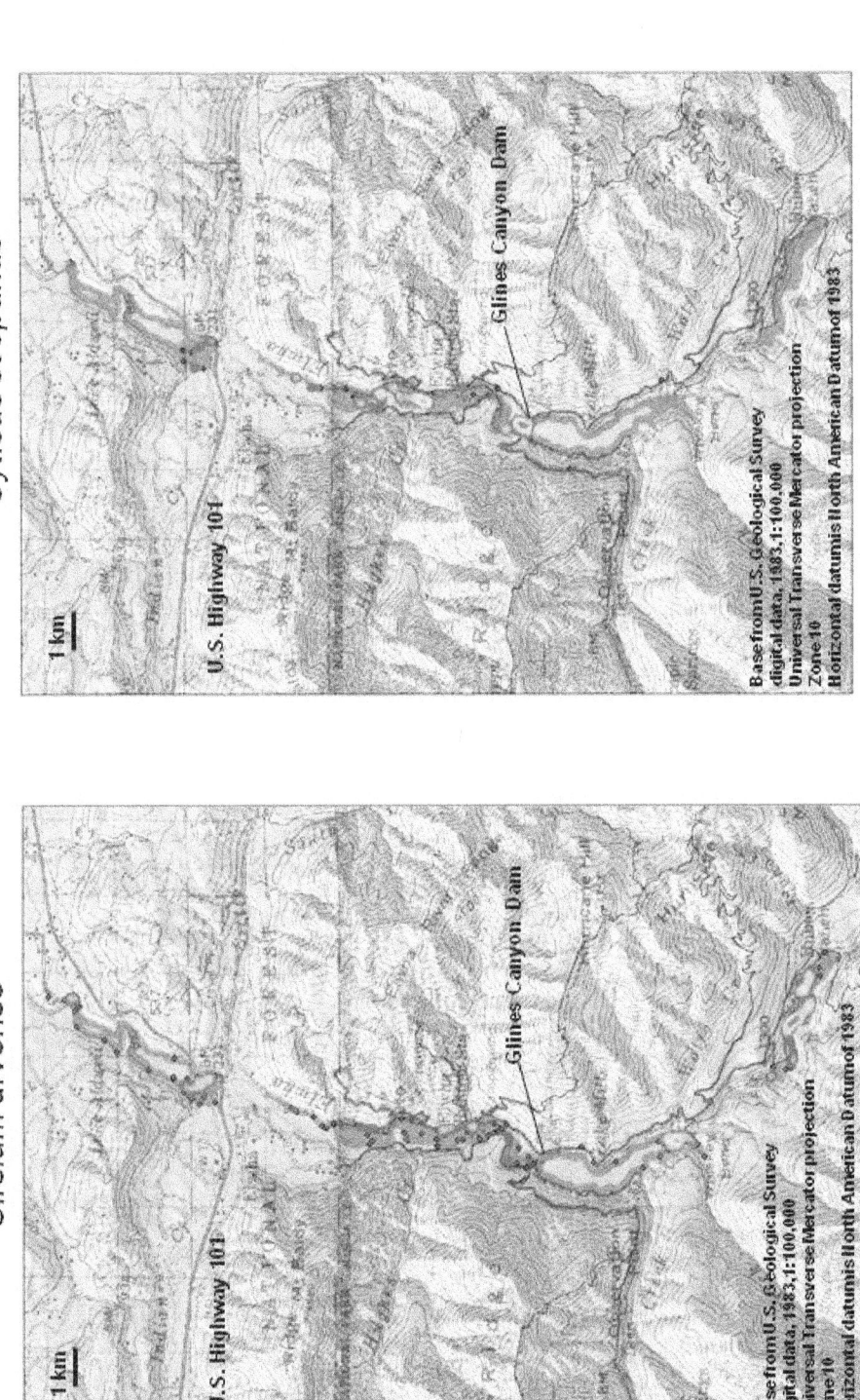

Figure 5. Kernel density representation of 'hot spots' of focal invasive species (high to low density represented by hot to cool colors), isolated observations (green points), and area surveyed during 2001 and 2008 (lilac), Elwha River, Olympic National Park, Washington.

27

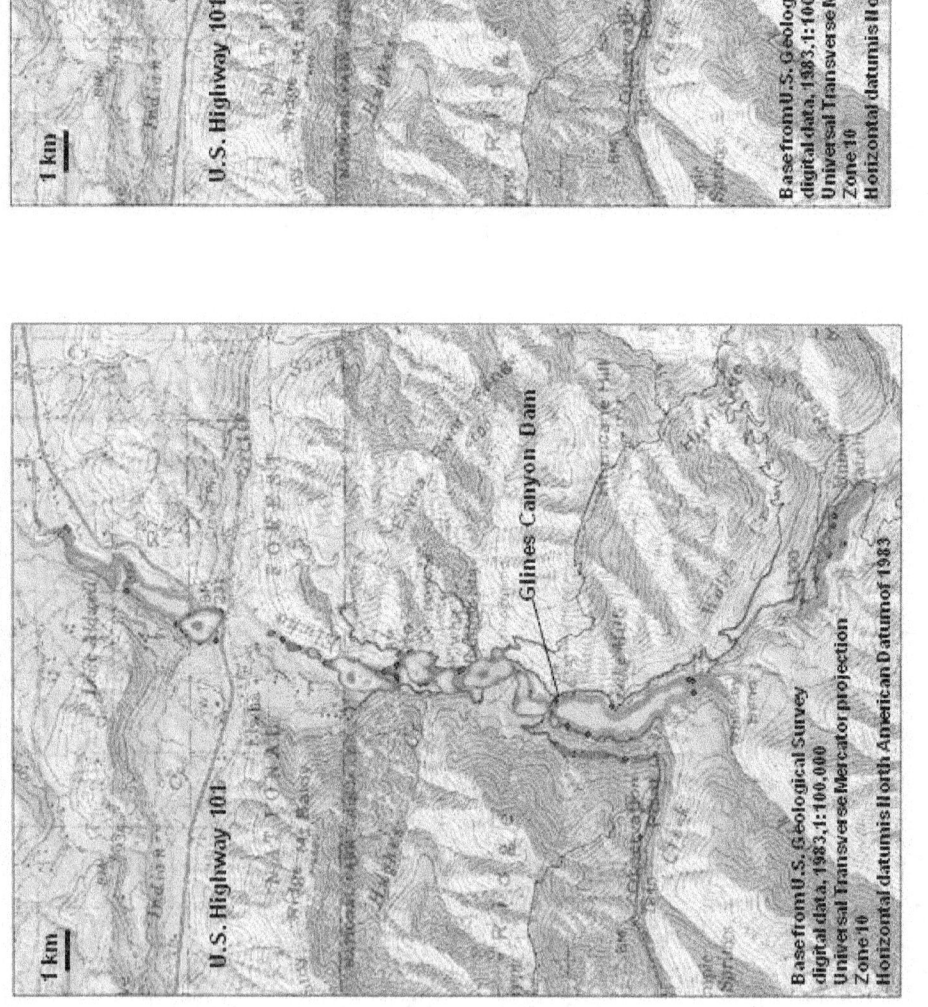

Figure 5. Kernel density representation of 'hot spots' of focal invasive species (high to low density represented by hot to cool colors), isolated observations (green points), and area surveyed during 2001 and 2008 (lilac), Elwha River, Olympic National Park, Washington.—Continued

Rubus spp.

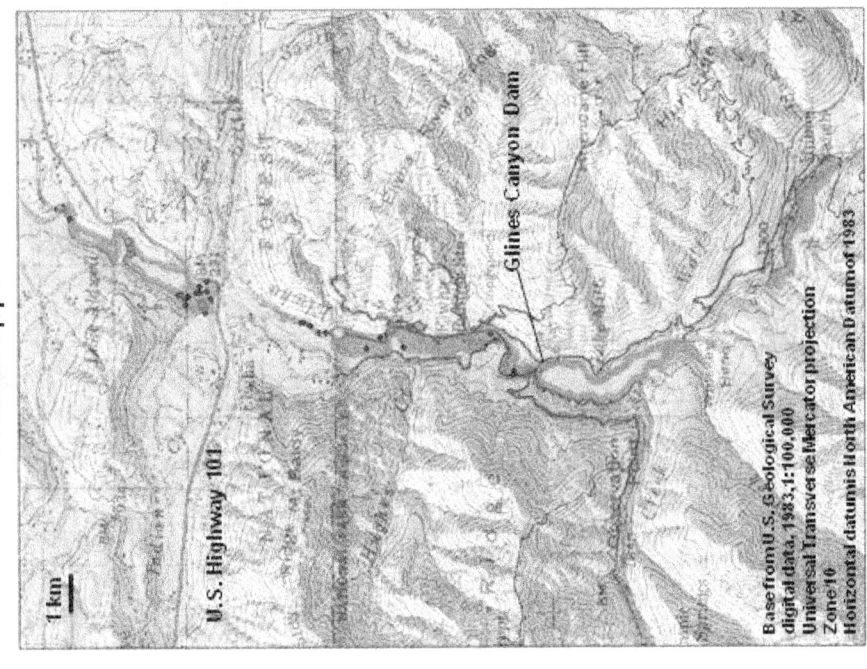

Figure 5. Kernel density representation of 'hot spots' of focal invasive species (high to low density represented by hot to cool colors), isolated observations (green points), and area surveyed during 2001 and 2008 (lilac), Elwha River, Olympic National Park, Washington.—Continued

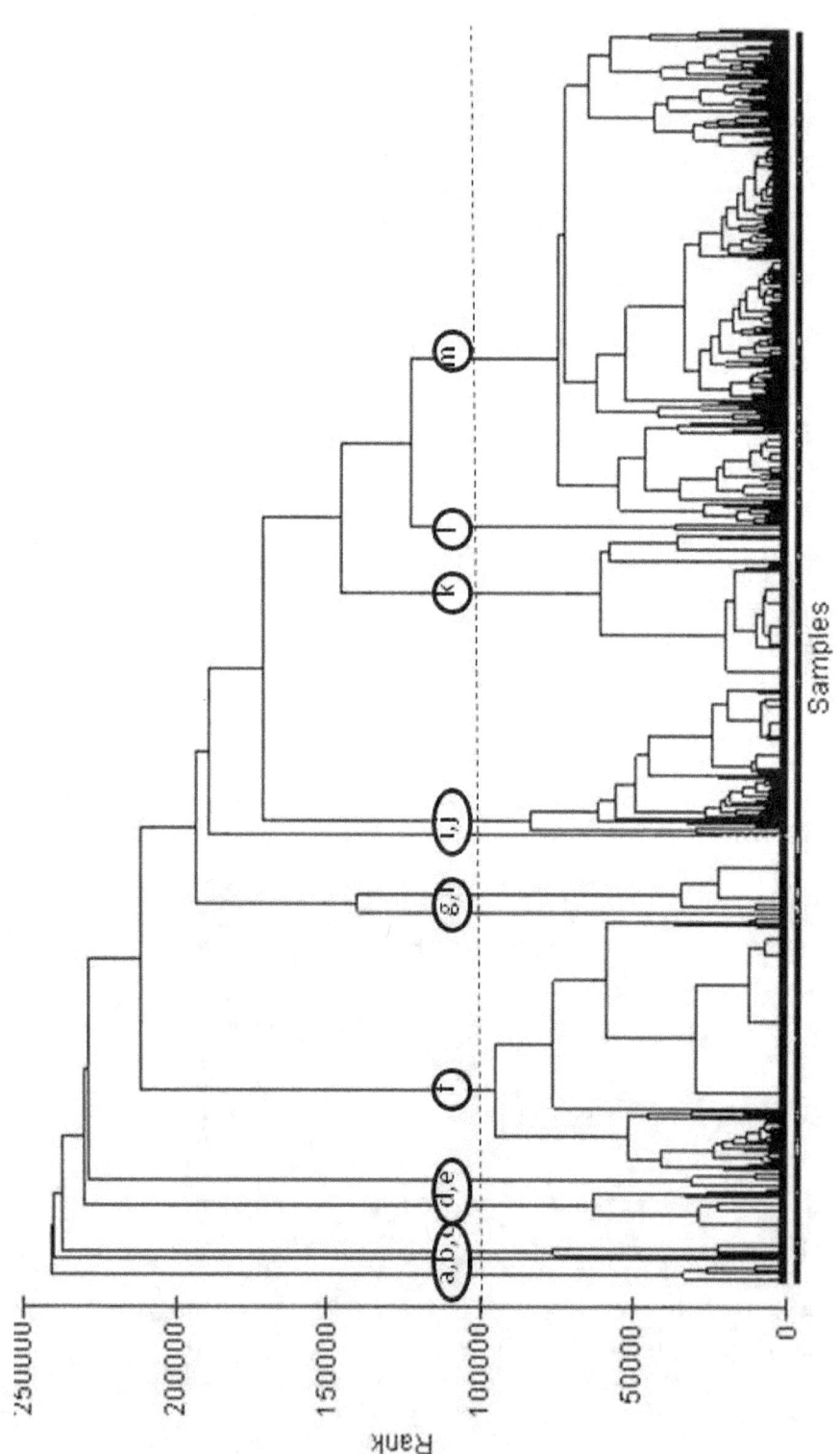

Figure 6. Cluster analysis of Bray-Curtis resemblances among survey sites. Groups that are indicated on ordination (fig. 7) are shown in circles. [Groups are dominated by: a, *Rubus* spp.; b, *Vicia* spp.; c, *Cytisus scoparius*; d, *Hypericum perforatum*; e, *Lathyrus sylvestris*; f, *Cirsium arvense*; g, *Rumex crispus*; h, *Cirsium vulgare*; i, *Arctium minus*; j, *Phalarus arundinacea*; k, *Geranium robertianum*; l, *Dactylis glomerata*; m, mixture of species]

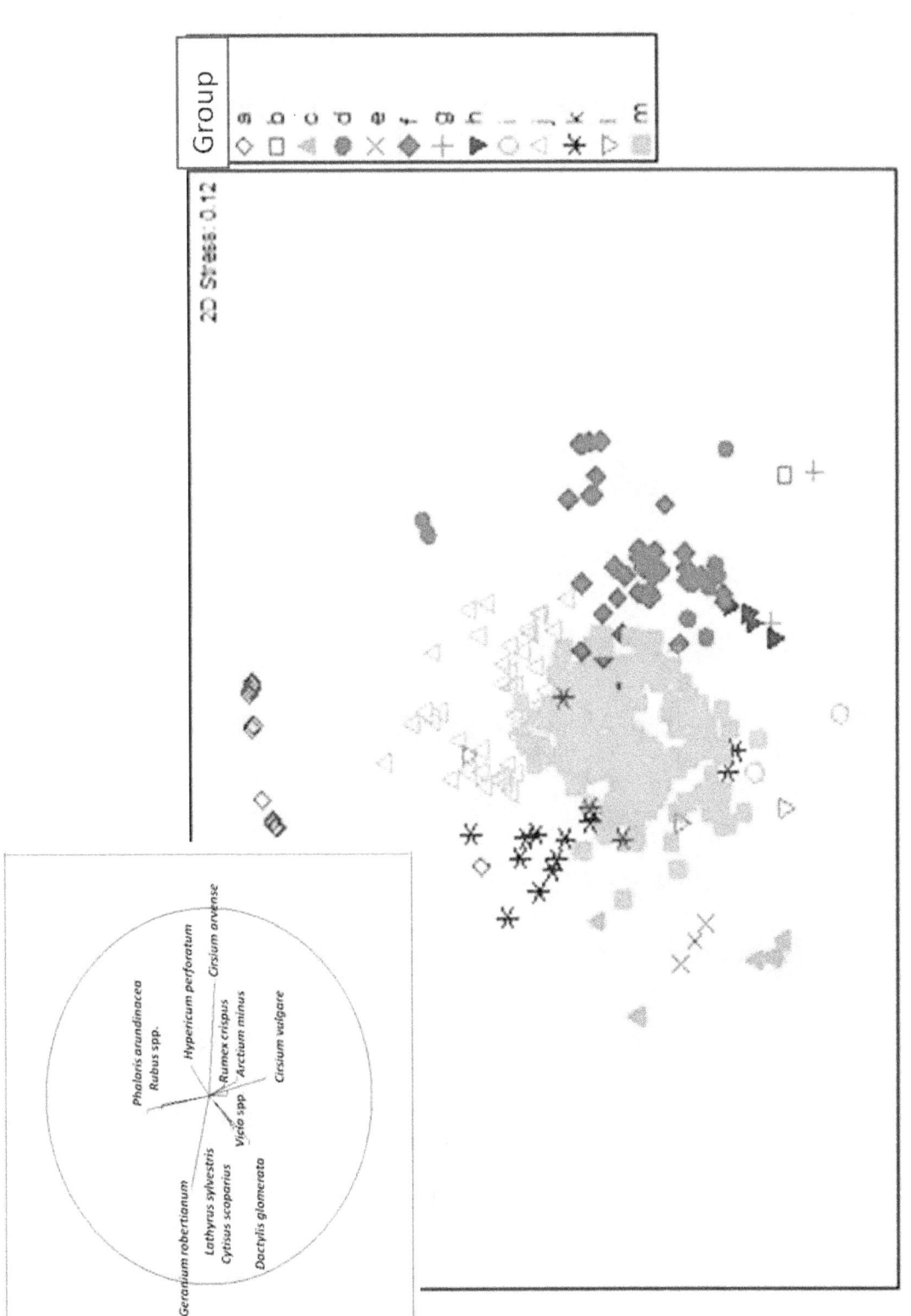

Figure 7. Non-metric multidimensional scaling ordination of sites. Ten groups labeled in figure 6 are indicated. The correlation of species abundance with dimensions of the ordination space are shown in the inset.

31

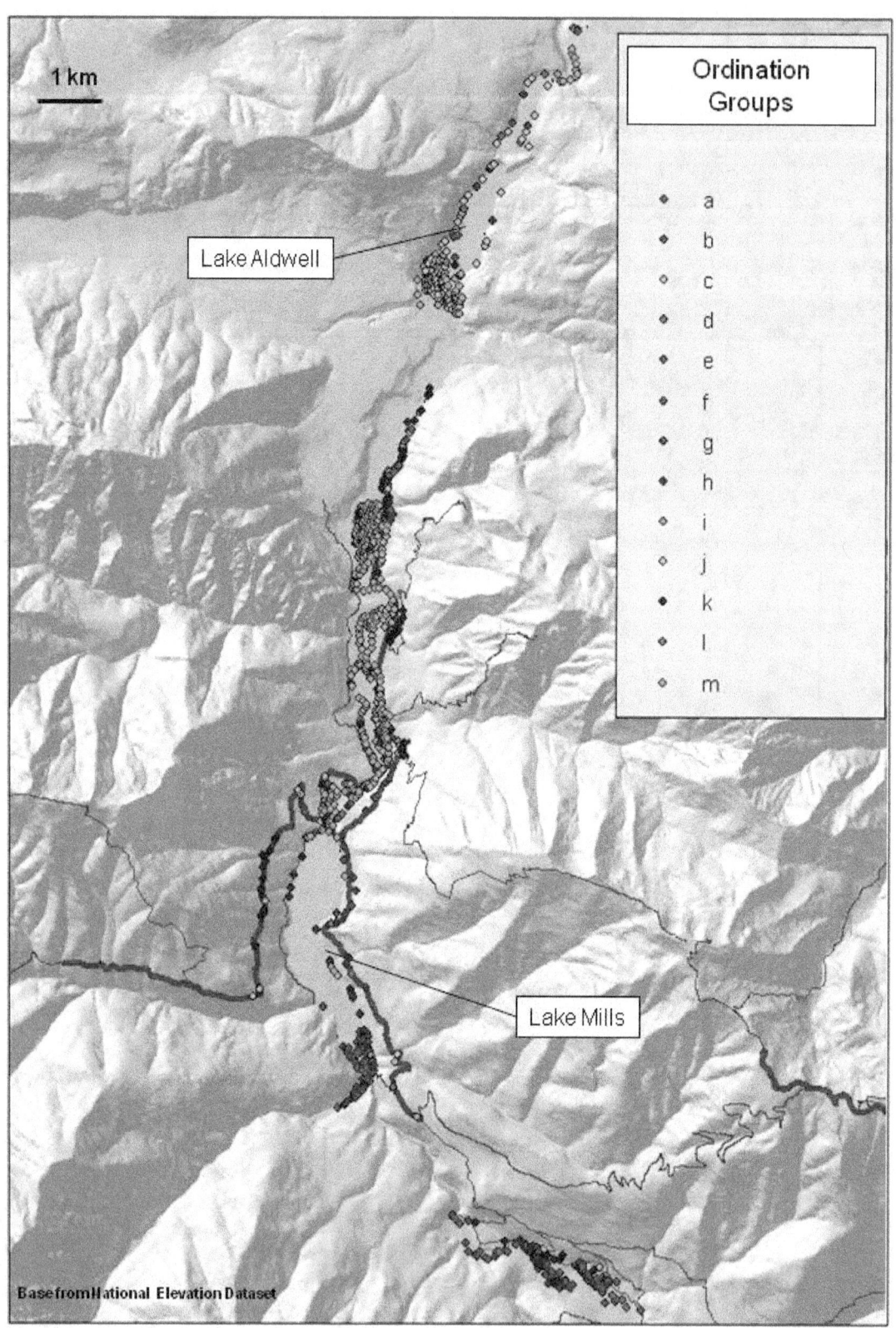

Figure 8. Locations of eleven ordination groups. Groups are defined in figure 6. Species dominating groups include *Rubus* spp. (a), *Vicia* spp. (b), *Cytisus scoparius* (c), *Hypericum perforatum* (d), *Lathyrus sylvestris* (e), *Cirsium arvense* (f), *Rumex crispus* (g), *Cirsium vulgare* (h), *Arctium minus* (i), *Phalaris arundinacea* (j), *Geranium robertianum* (k), *Dactylis glomeratt* (l) and mixed species (m).

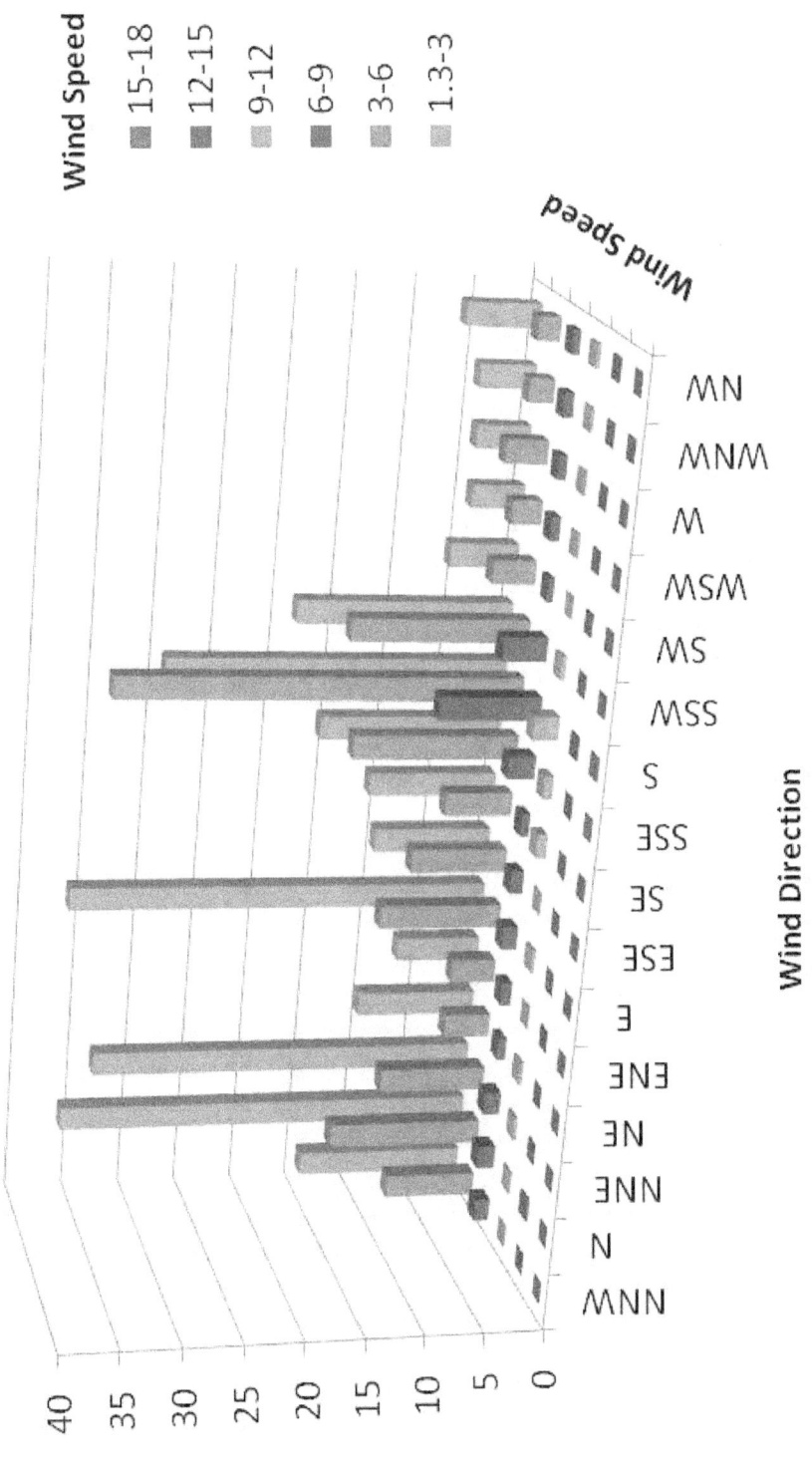

Figure 9. Summary of distribution of wind speed and direction (source) from RAWS station at Hurricane Ridge. The vertical axis represents percentage of time at each speed and direction accumulated over 10 years (1999–2008).

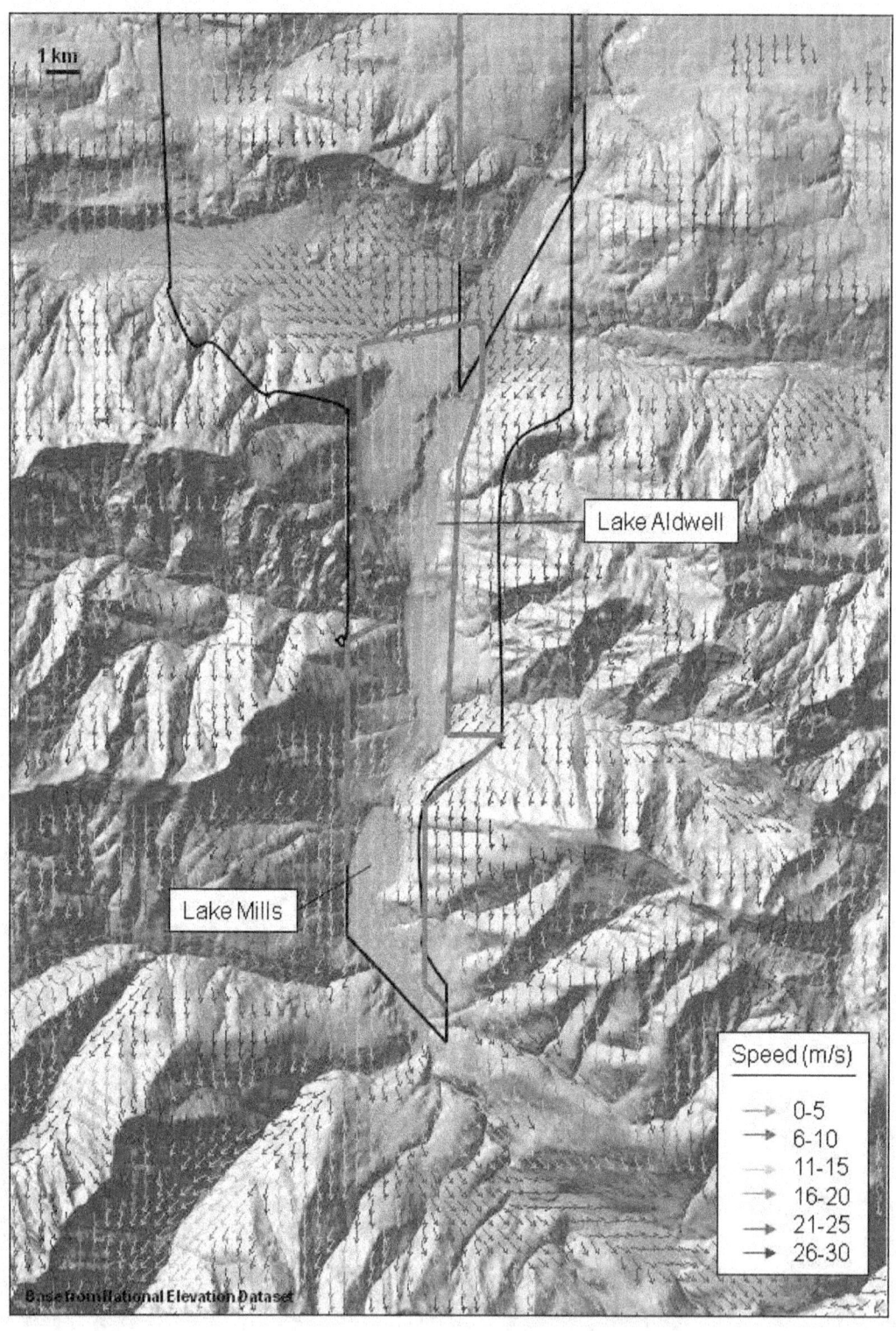

Figure 10. Effect of topography on wind measured at 15 m/s from the north at the Hurricane Ridge RAWS station predicted by WindNinja (Forthofer, 2007). All sources areas are outlined in black; high priority source areas are outlined in green.

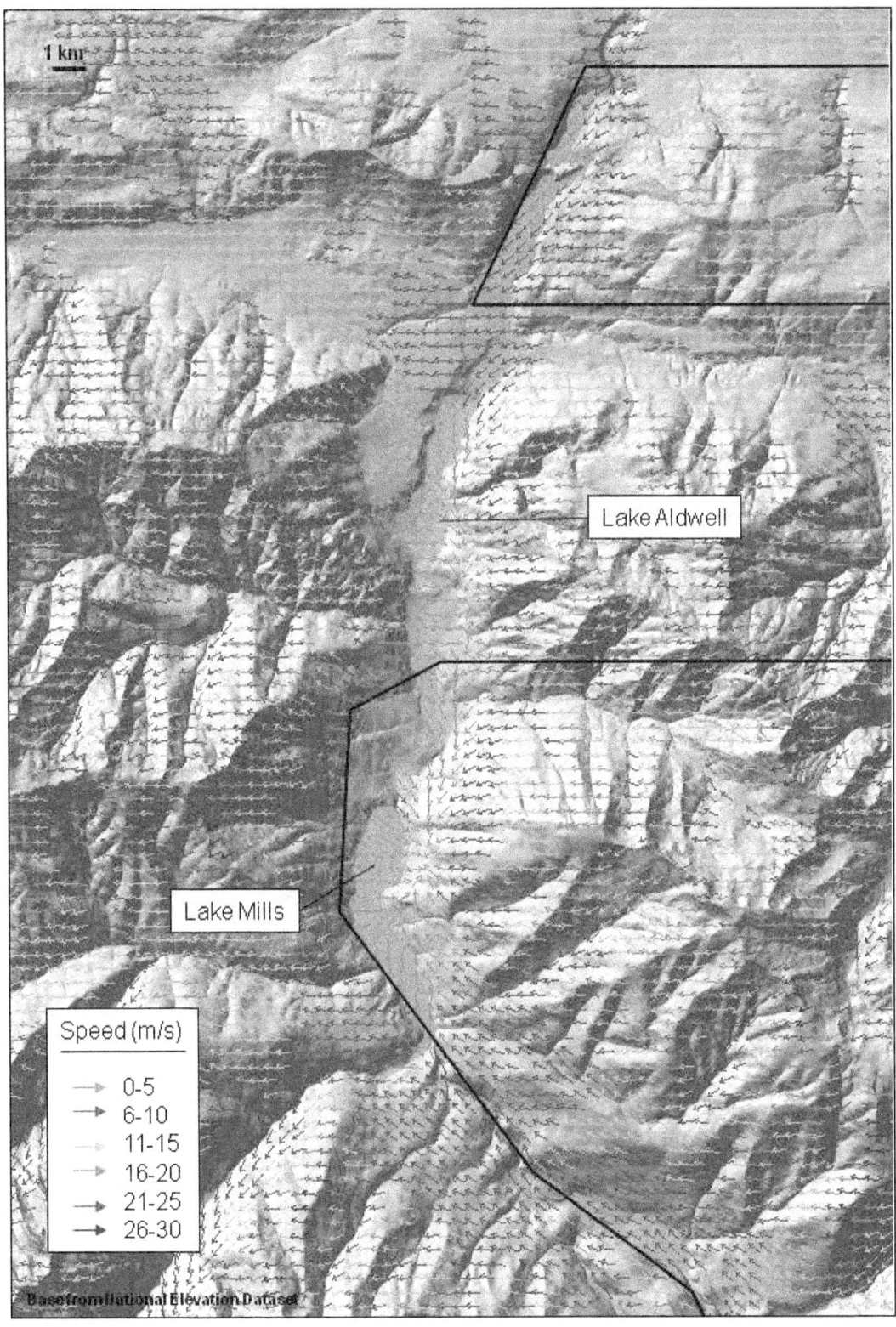

Figure 11. Effect of topography on wind measured at 12 m/s from the east at the Hurricane Ridge RAWS station predicted by WindNinja (Forthofer, 2007). All sources areas are outlined in black.

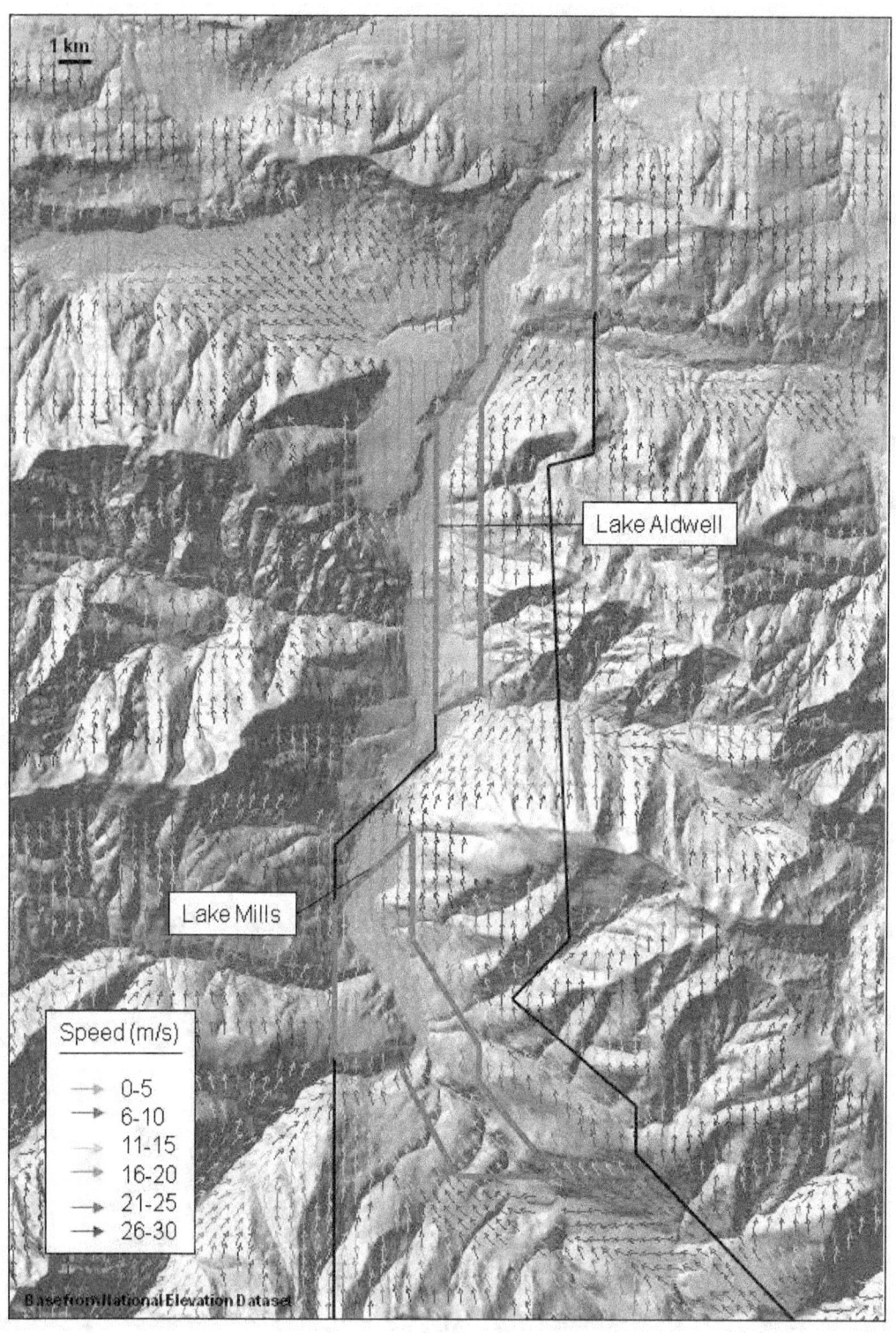

Figure 12. Effect of topography on wind measured at 18 m/s from the south at the Hurricane Ridge RAWS station predicted by WindNinja (Forthofer, 2007). All sources areas are outlined in black; high priority source areas are outlined in green.

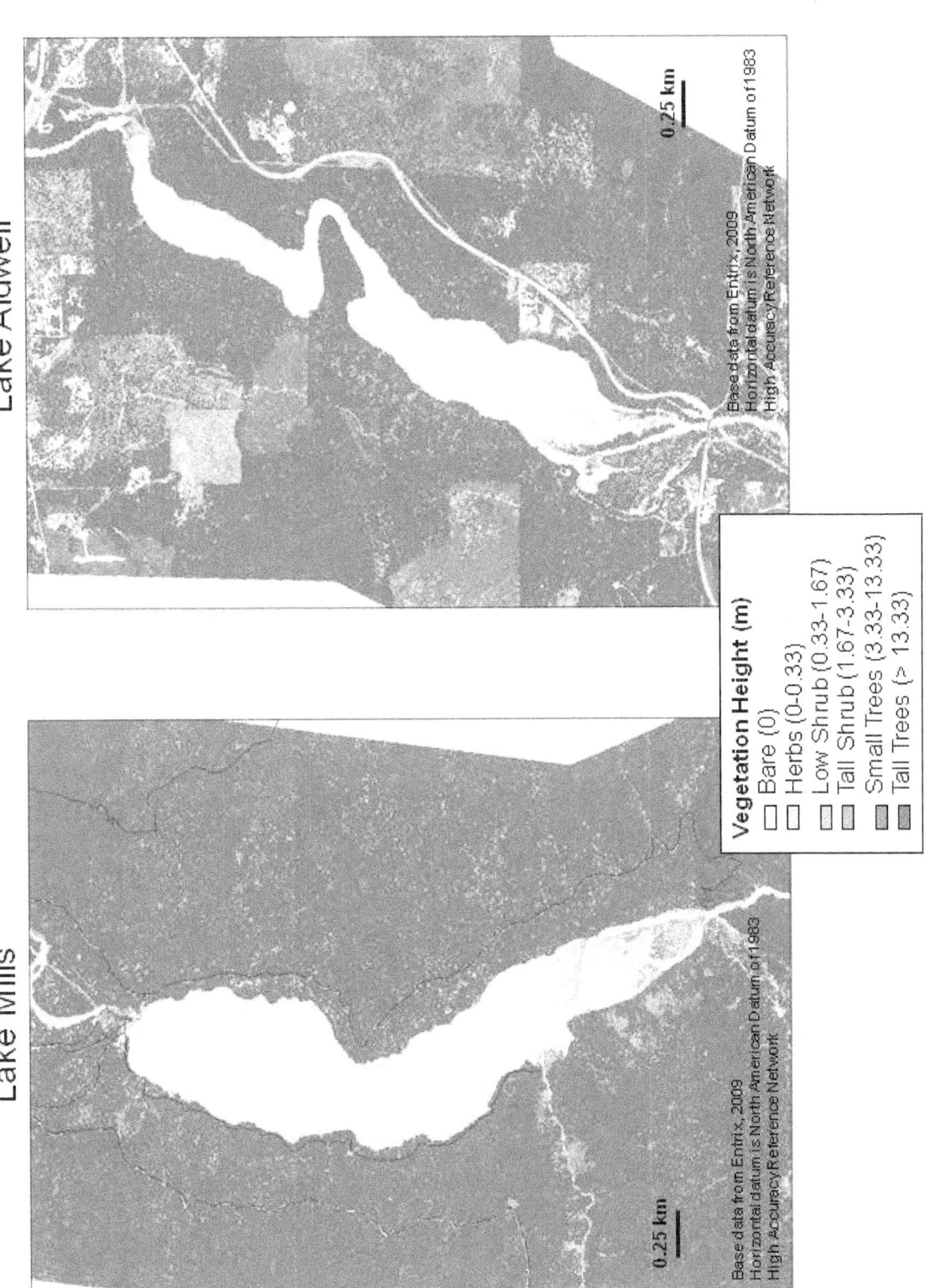

Figure 13. Vegetation height surrounding Lake Mills and Lake Aldwell reservoirs based on LiDAR data.

37

Cirsium arvense

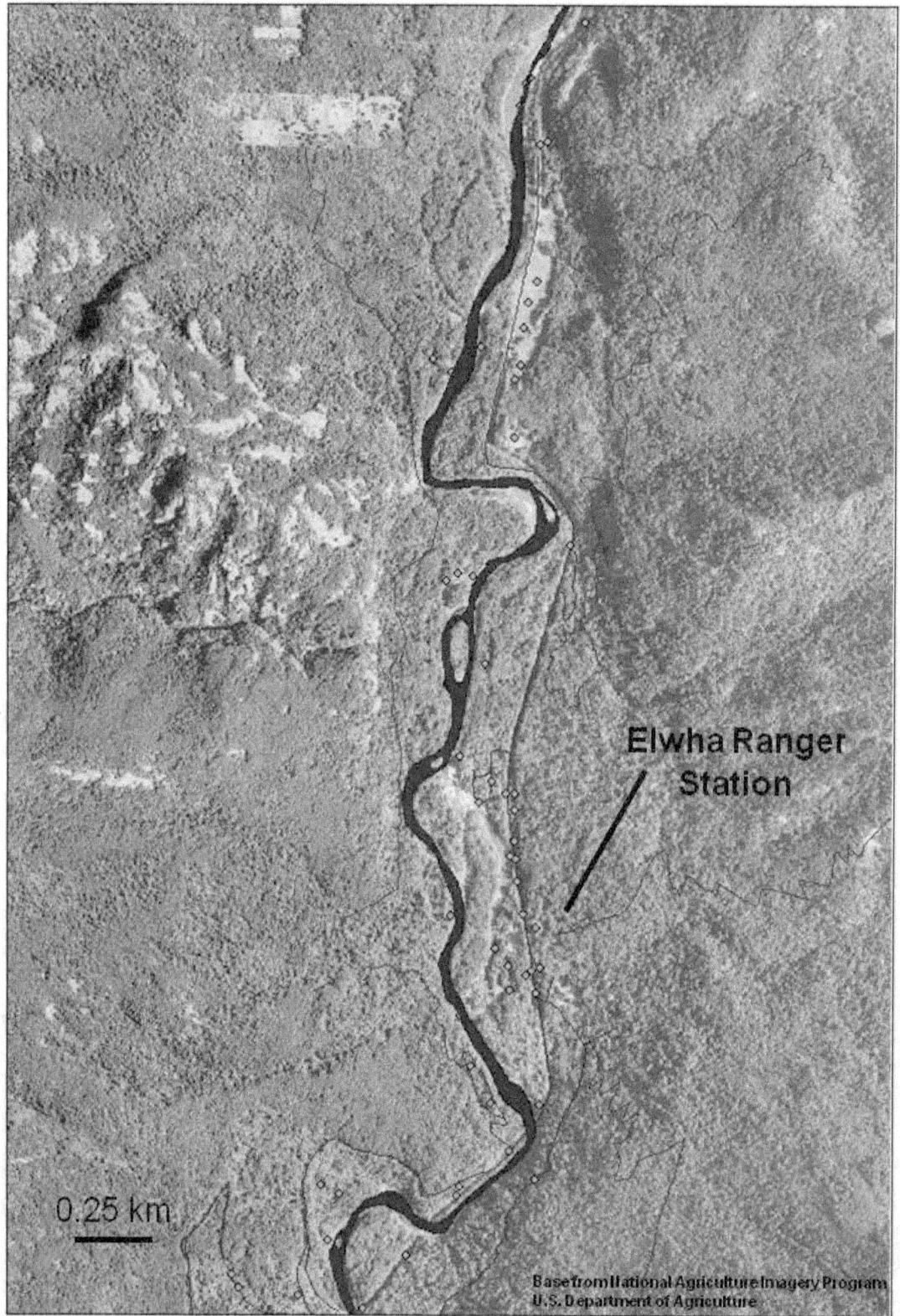

Figure 14. Species with distribution patterns consistent with water dispersal. Area shown is approximately between the park boundary and Glines Canyon Dam.

Cytisus scoparius

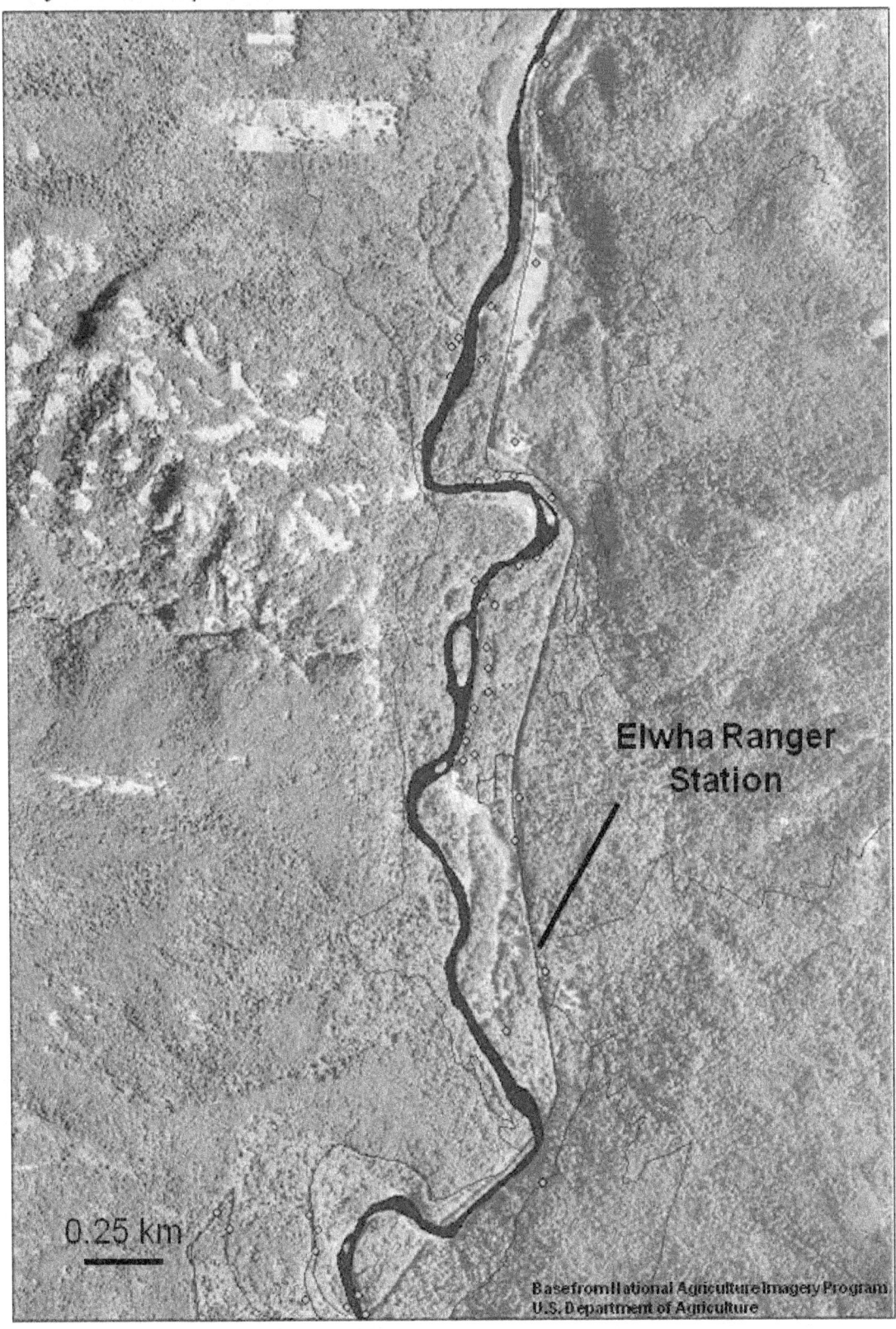

Figure 14. Species with distribution patterns consistent with water dispersal.—Continued. Area shown is approximately between the park boundary and Glines Canyon Dam.

Geranium robertianum

Figure 14. Species with distribution patterns consistent with water dispersal.—Continued. Area shown is approximately between the park boundary and Glines Canyon Dam.

Lathyrus sylvestris

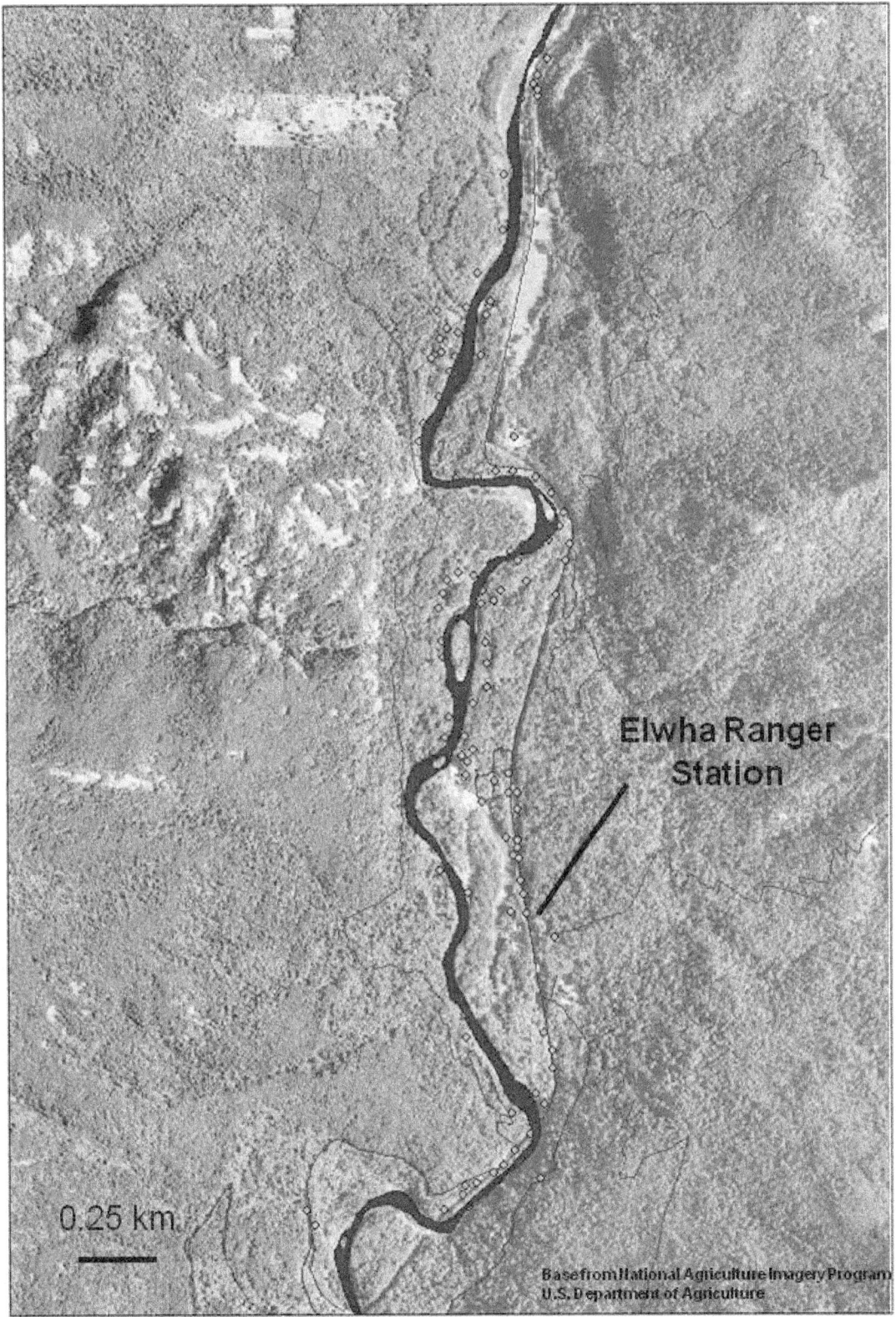

Figure 14. Species with distribution patterns consistent with water dispersal.—Continued. Area shown is approximately between the park boundary and Glines Canyon Dam.

Phalaris arundinacea

Figure 14. Species with distribution patterns consistent with water dispersal.—Continued. Area shown is approximately between the park boundary and Glines Canyon Dam.

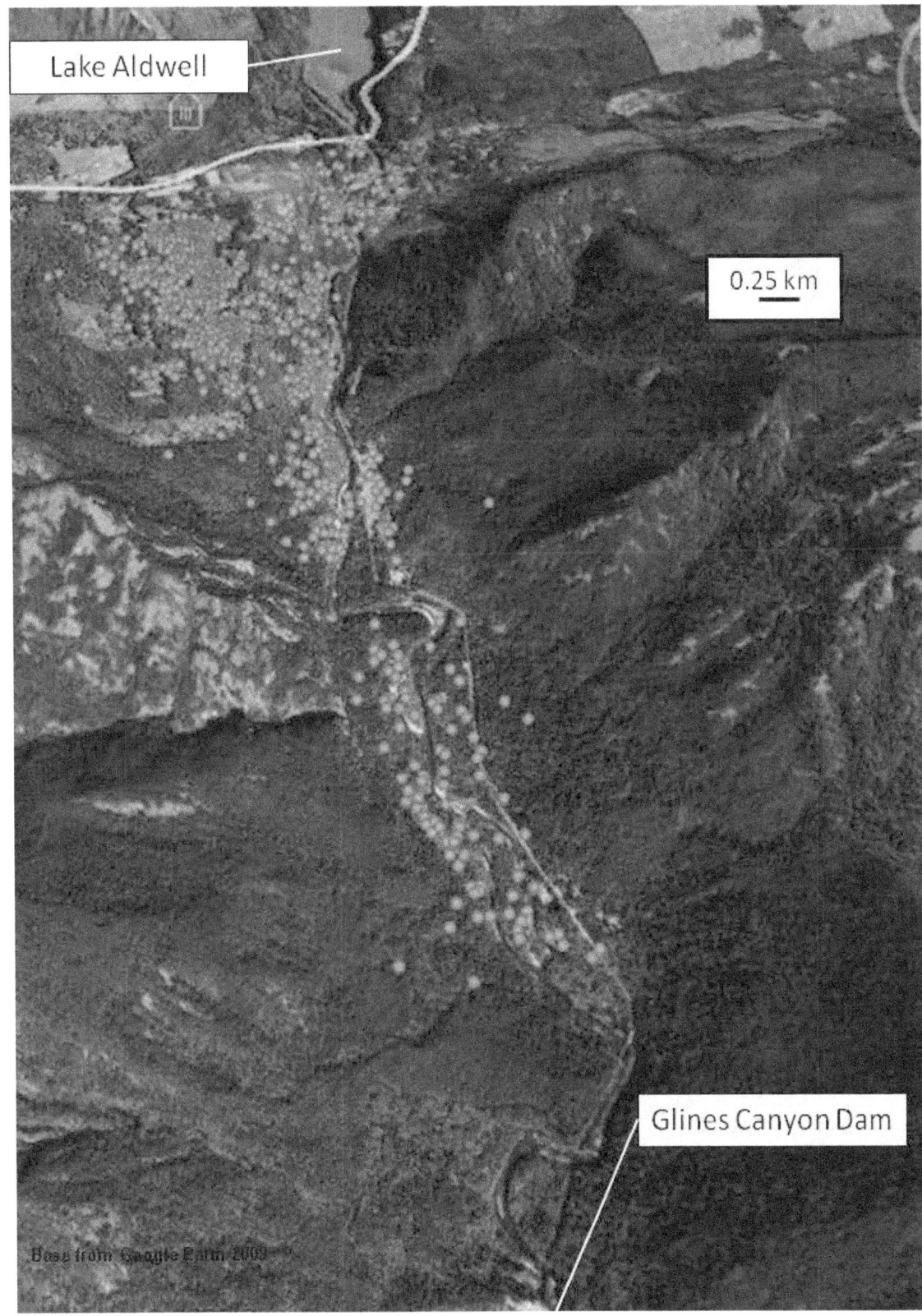

Figure 15. Locations of one radio collared elk tracked by the Lower Elwha Klallam Tribe from February 2009 to November 2009. Points represent six observations per day.

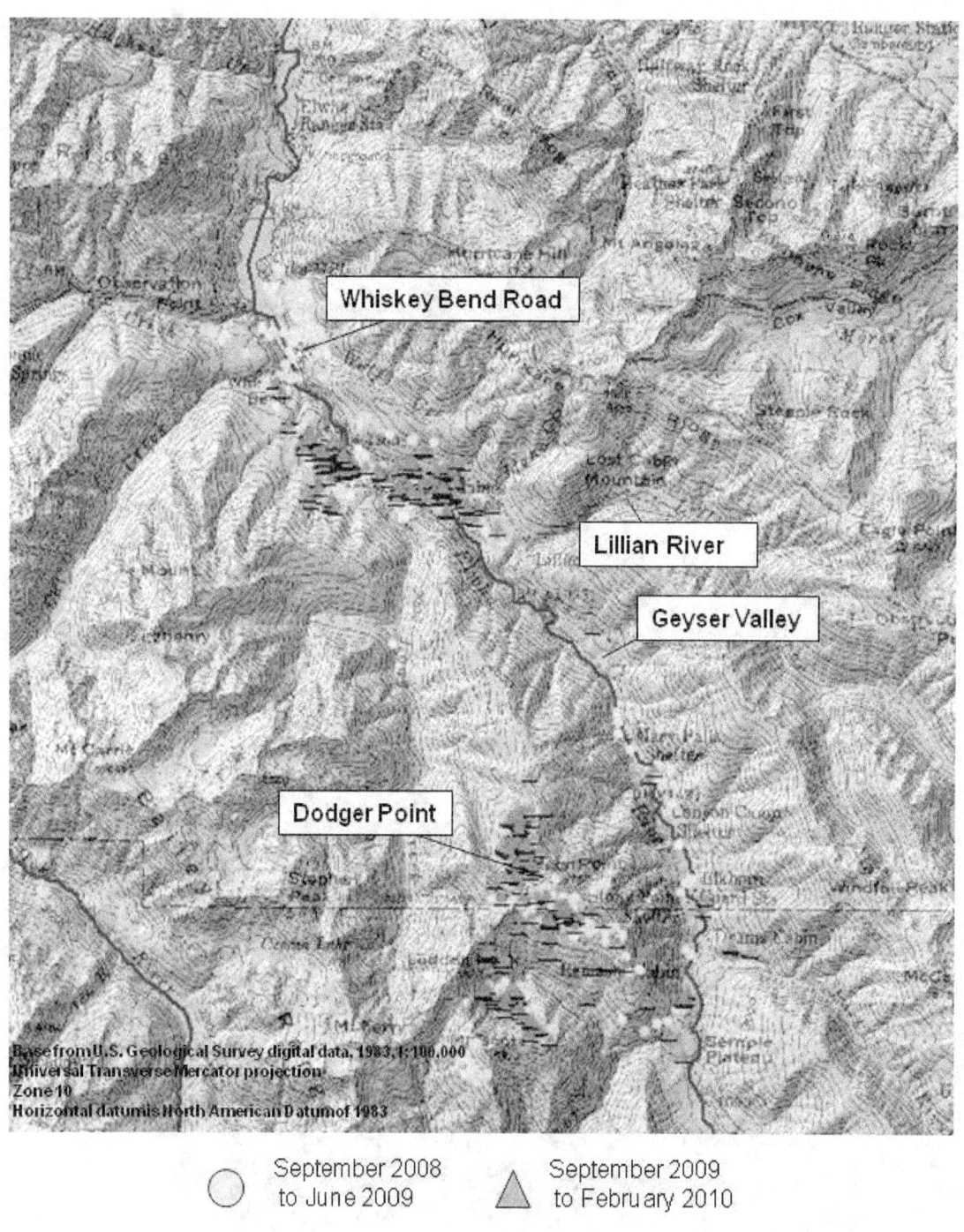

Figure 16. Locations of two radio-collared elk tracked by Olympic National Park staff, one from September 2008 to June 2009, and one from September 2009 to February 2010. Points represent four observations per day.

Beaver sign: ☐ Likely ▨ Observed

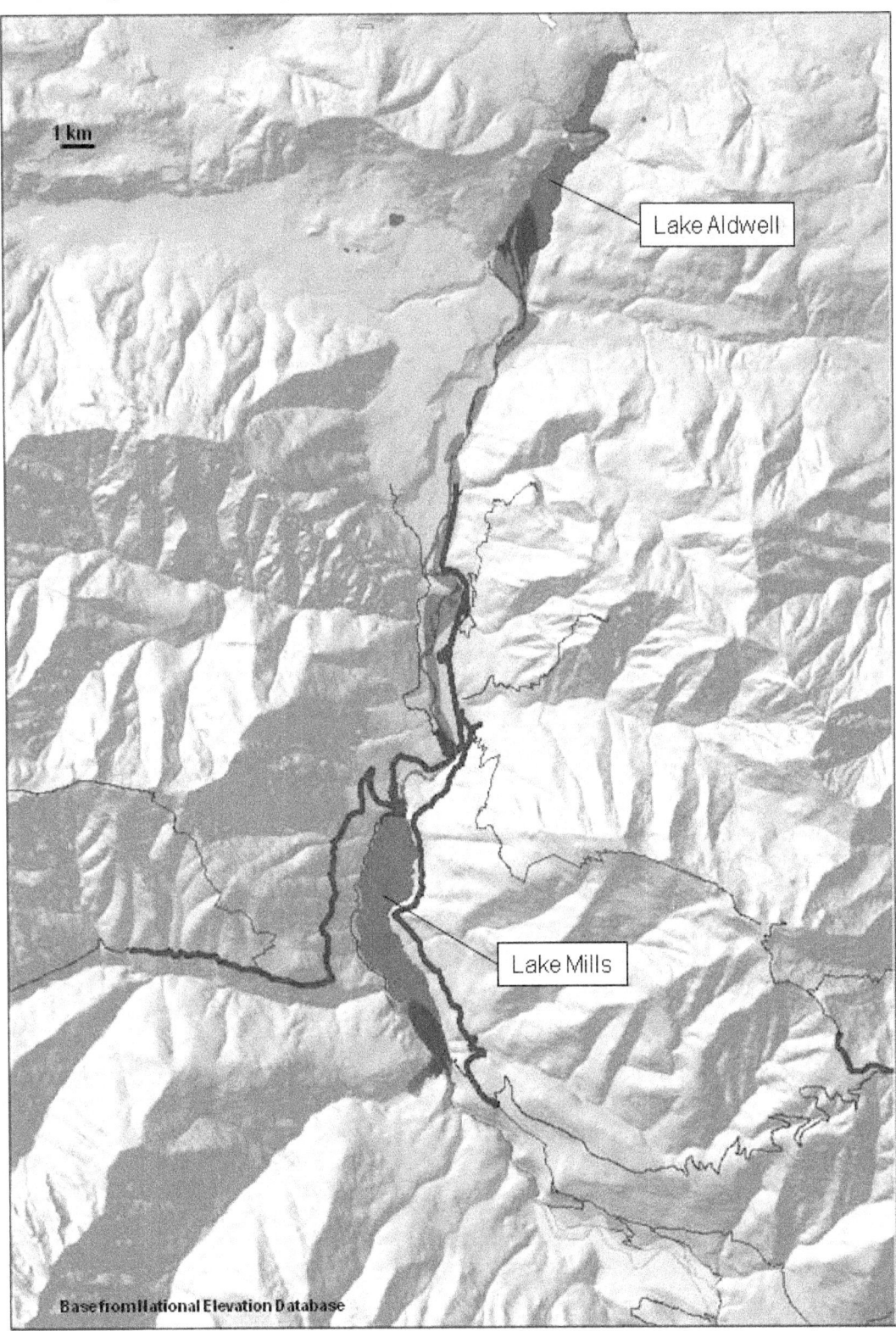

Figure 17. Locations of observed and likely beaver sign, Elwha River, Olympic National Park, Washington, 2007 (redrawn from Knapp, 2009).

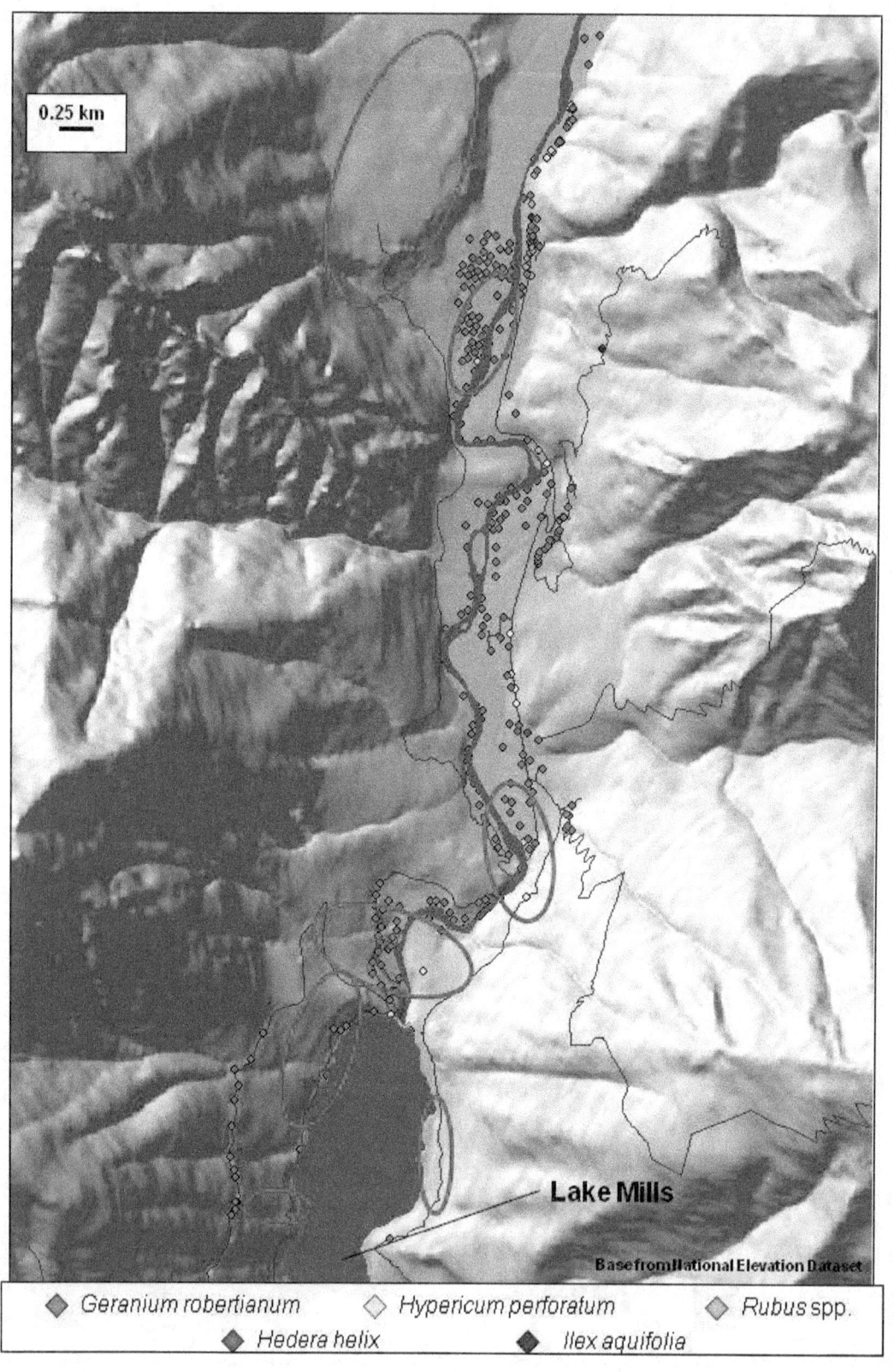

Figure 18. Distribution of most likely bird-dispersed invasive plant species compared with highest densities of most likely avian dispersers (red ovals), Elwha River, Olympic National Park, Washington.

46

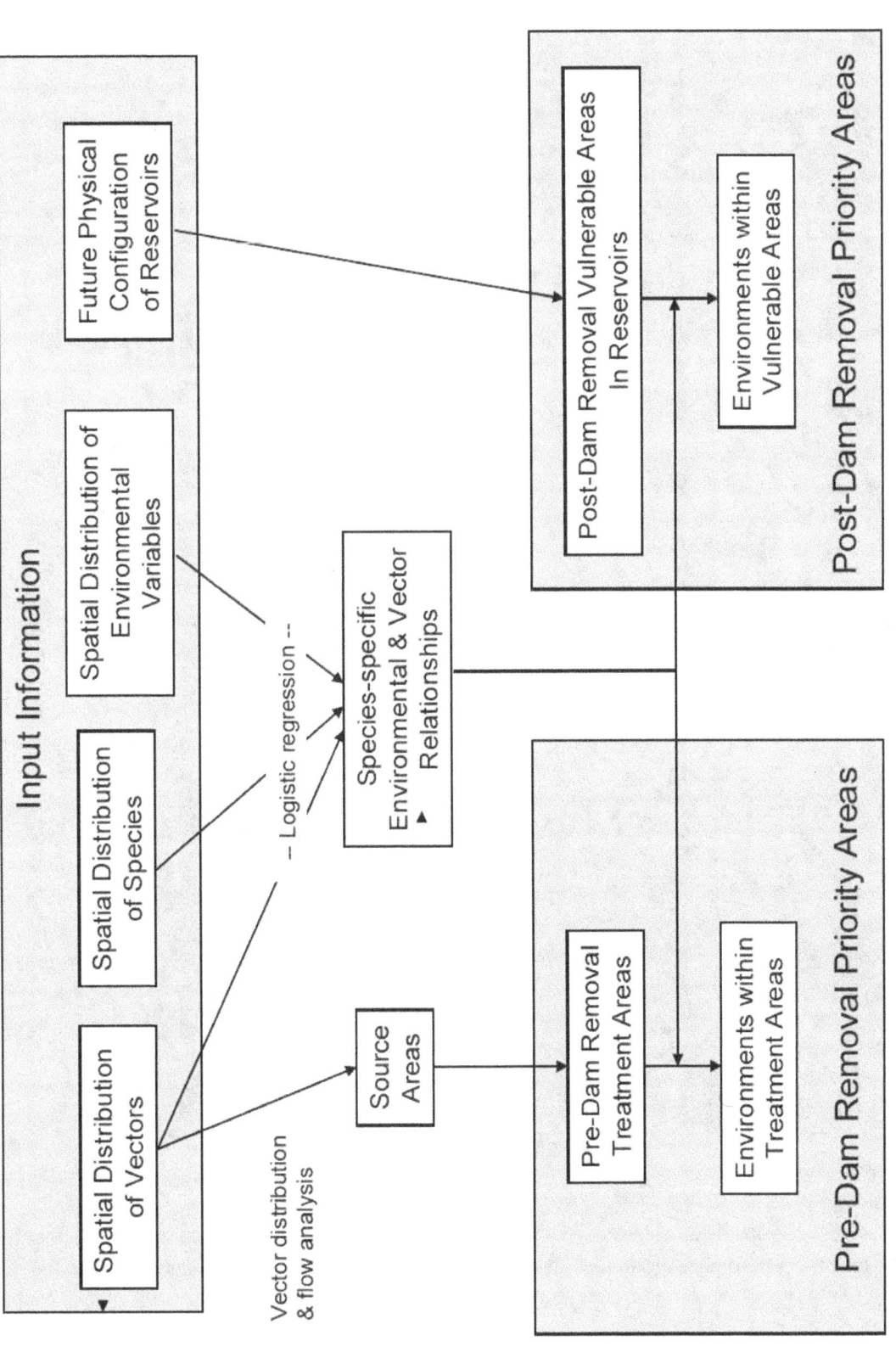

Figure 19. Schematic description of the approach to identifying areas and environments within areas that should be treated for invasive plant species prior to dam removal and that will be vulnerable to invasion after dam removal.

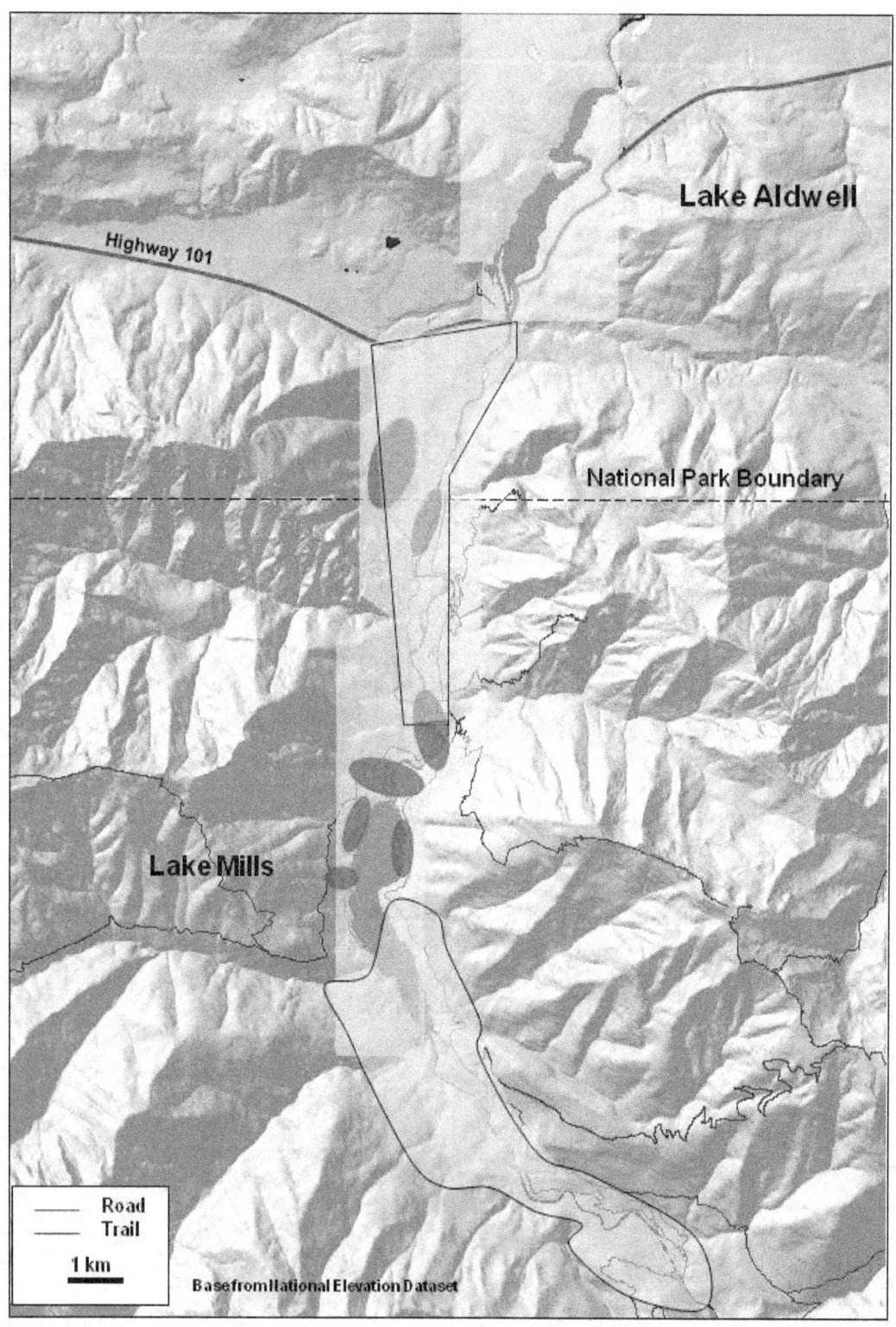

Figure 20. Potential source areas of vectors of invasive species that could impact the de-watered reservoirs. Source areas are designated for wind (yellow), birds (orange), and mammals (blue). Locations of roads and trails also are indicated.

48

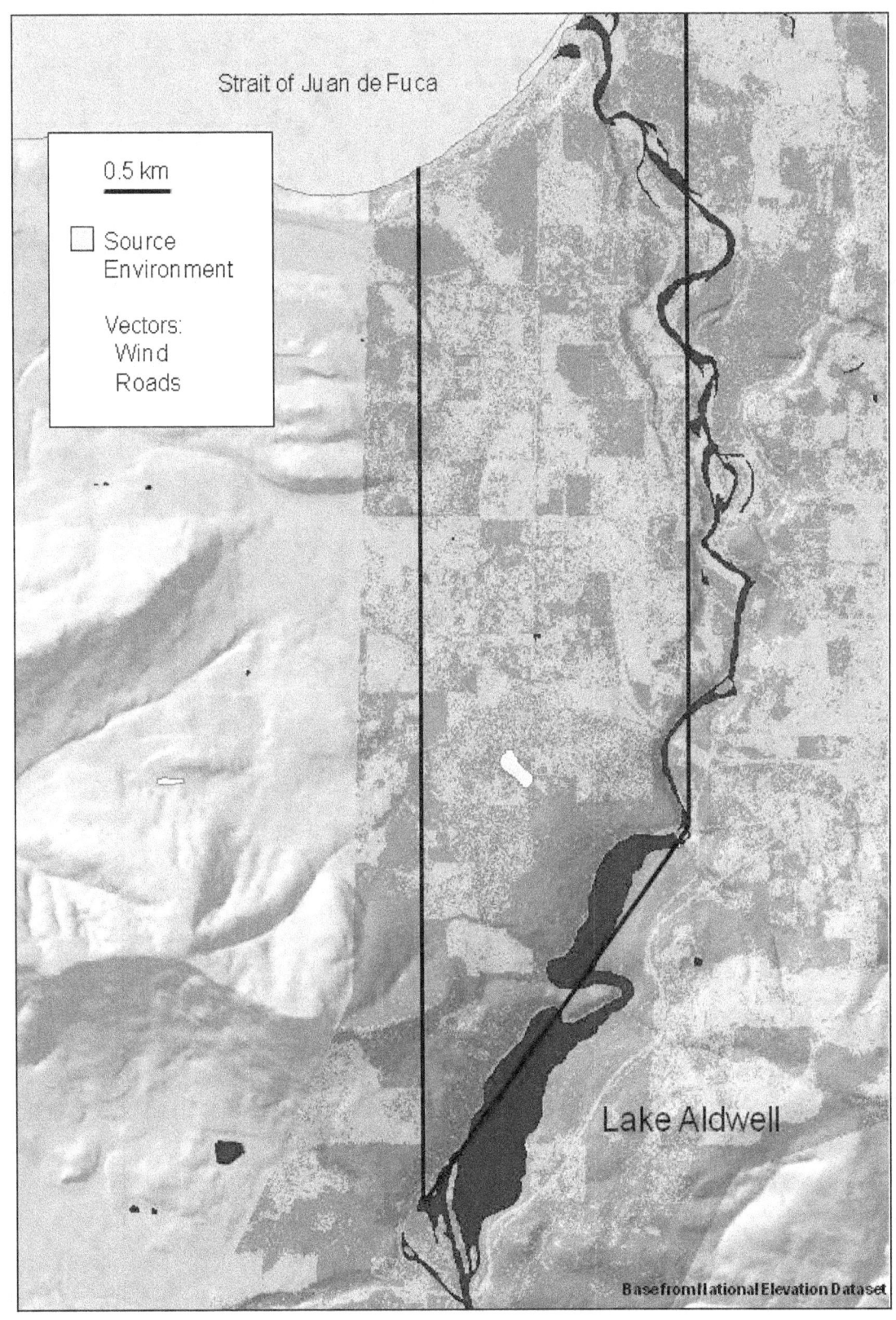

Figure 21. Environments (green within black lines) where *C. arvense* is most likely to occur north of Lake Aldwell.

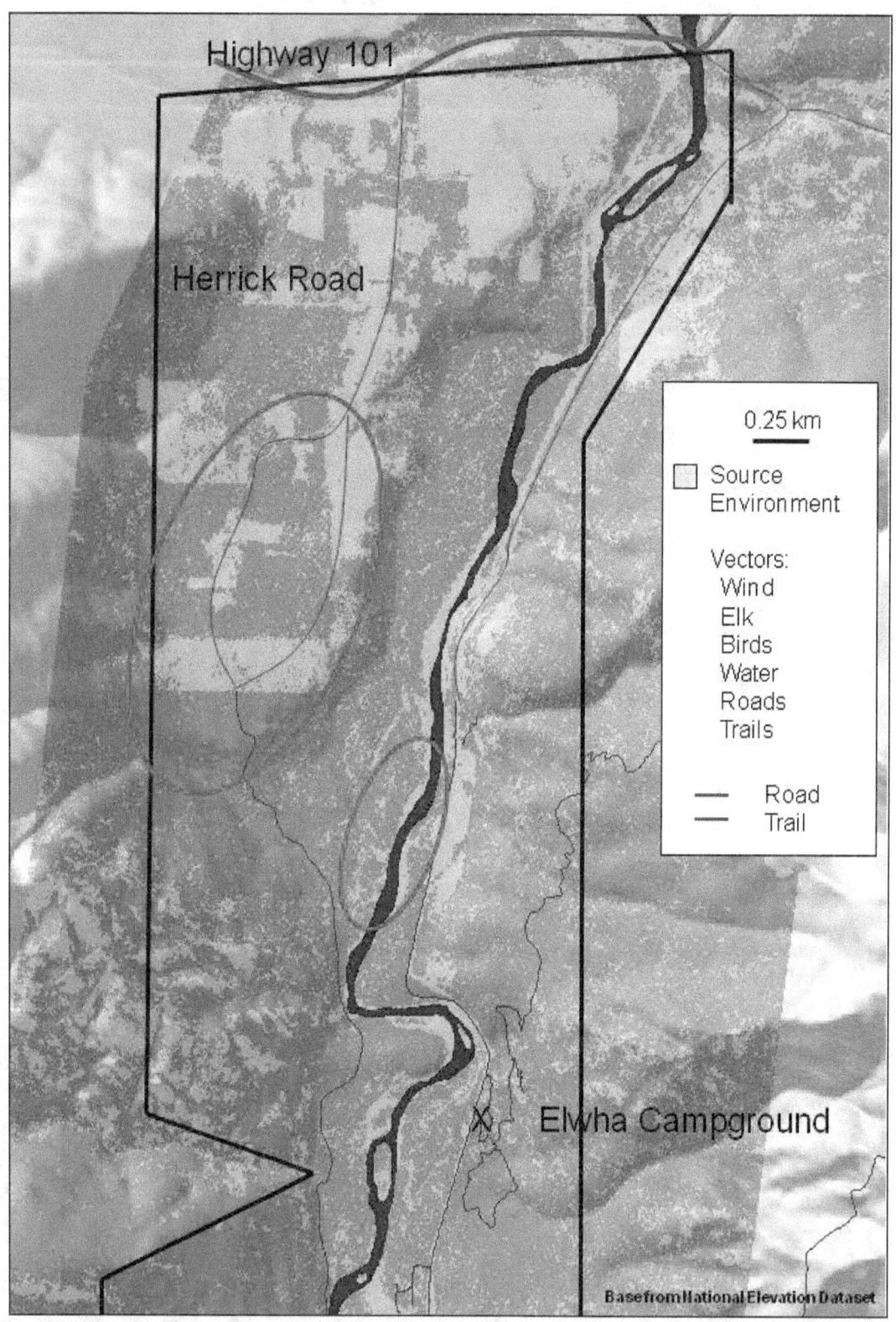

Figure 22. Environments that are potential sources of invasive species (green areas within black lines) in the area south of Lake Aldwell to the Elwha Campground. *Hedera helix* and *Ilex aquifolia* located within the red ovals has a high potential to be spread by birds.

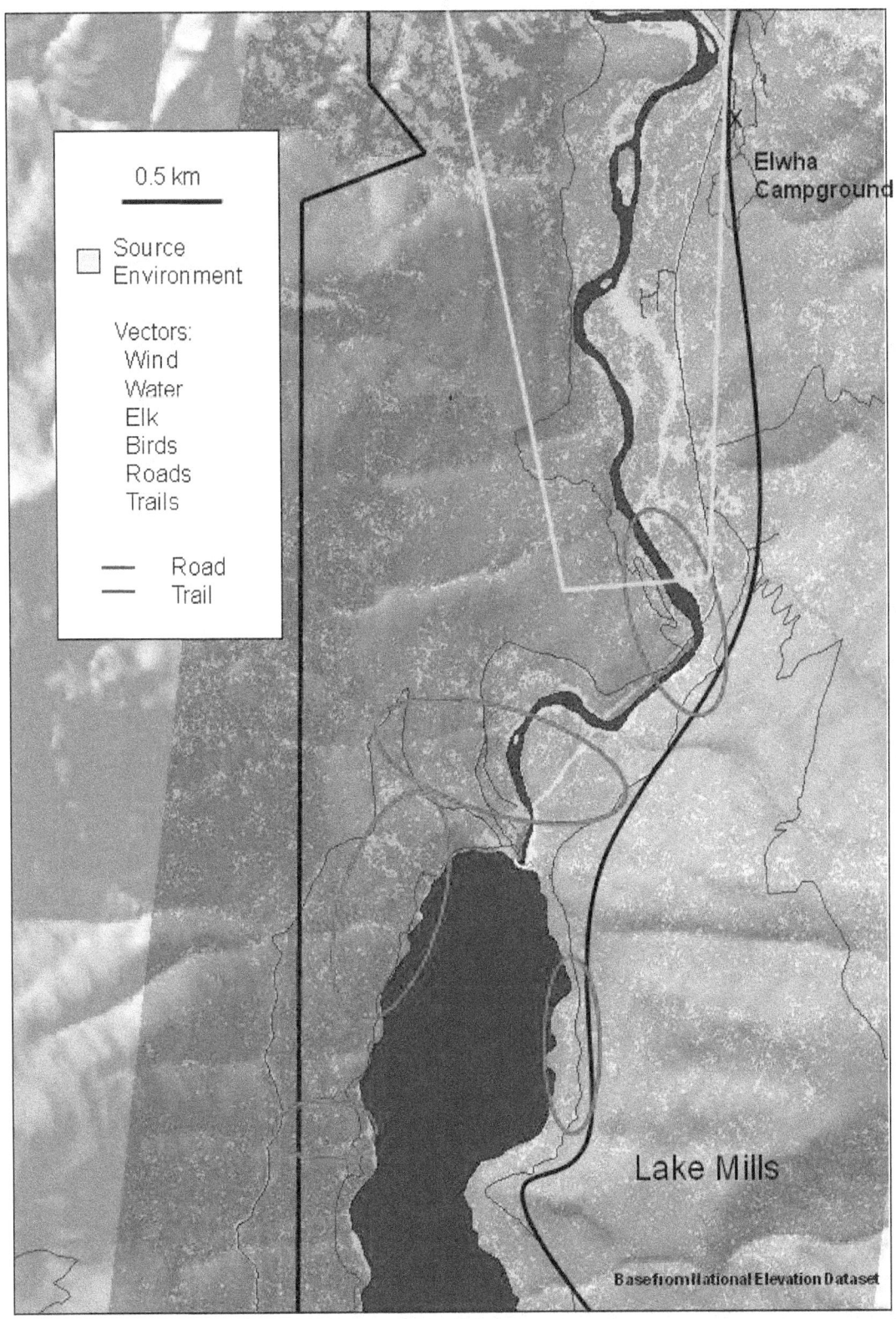

Figure 23. Environments that are potential sources of invasive plants (green areas within black lines) between Elwha Campground and Lake Mills. Areas where birds (red ovals) and elk (blue lines) are active are also indicated. (Put blue and red lines in key.)

Figure 24. Environments that are potential sources of invasive plants (green areas within black lines) along Lake Mills up to Geyser Valley. Besides roads and trails, elk and wind are the most important vectors in this area.

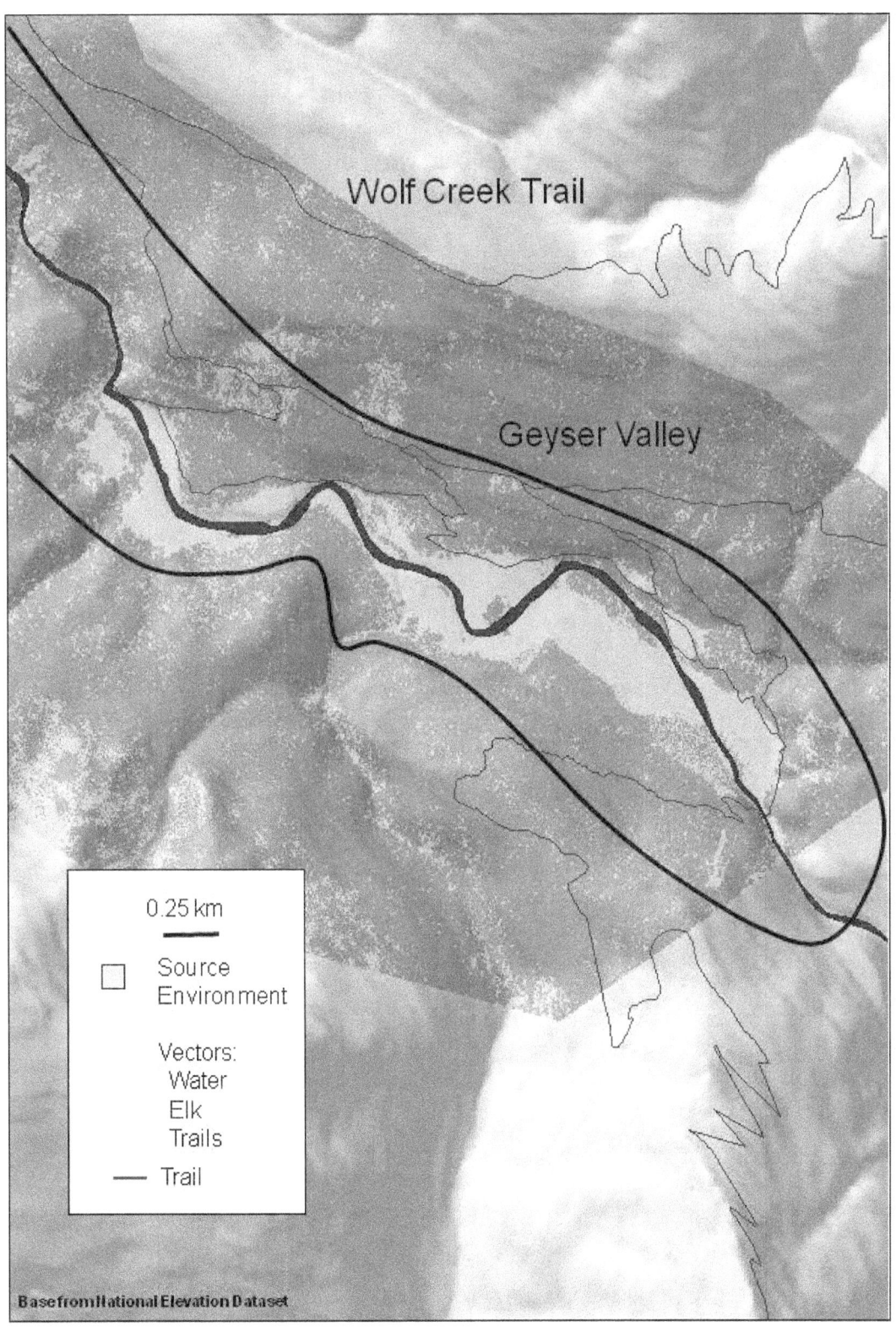

Figure 25. Environments that are potential sources of invasive plants (green areas within black lines) in Geyser Valley. Elk and trail users are the most likely vectors to spread invasive plants to the de-watered reservoirs.

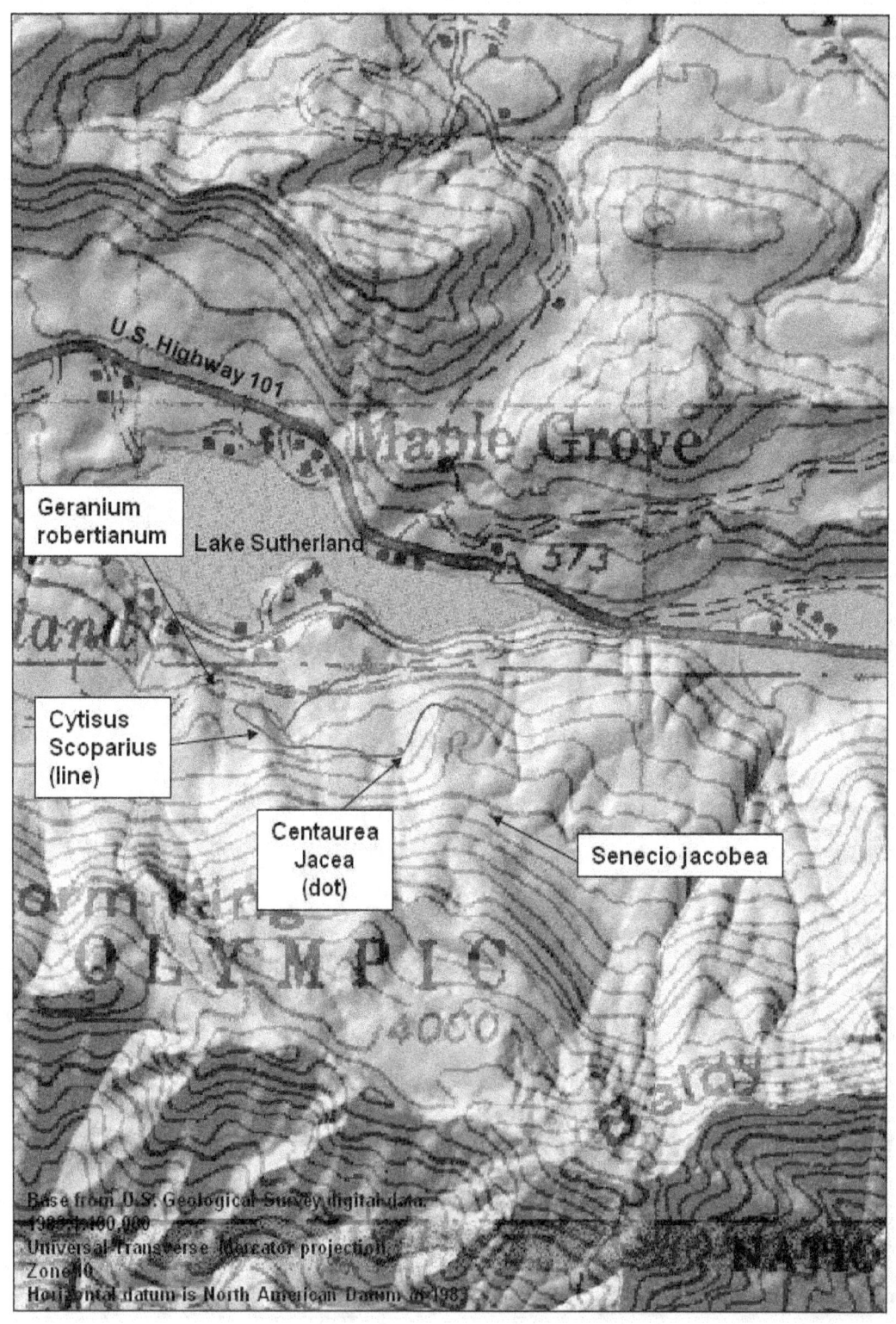

Figure 26. Digitized records of invasive plants on the Olympic National Forest, west of the Elwha reservoirs.

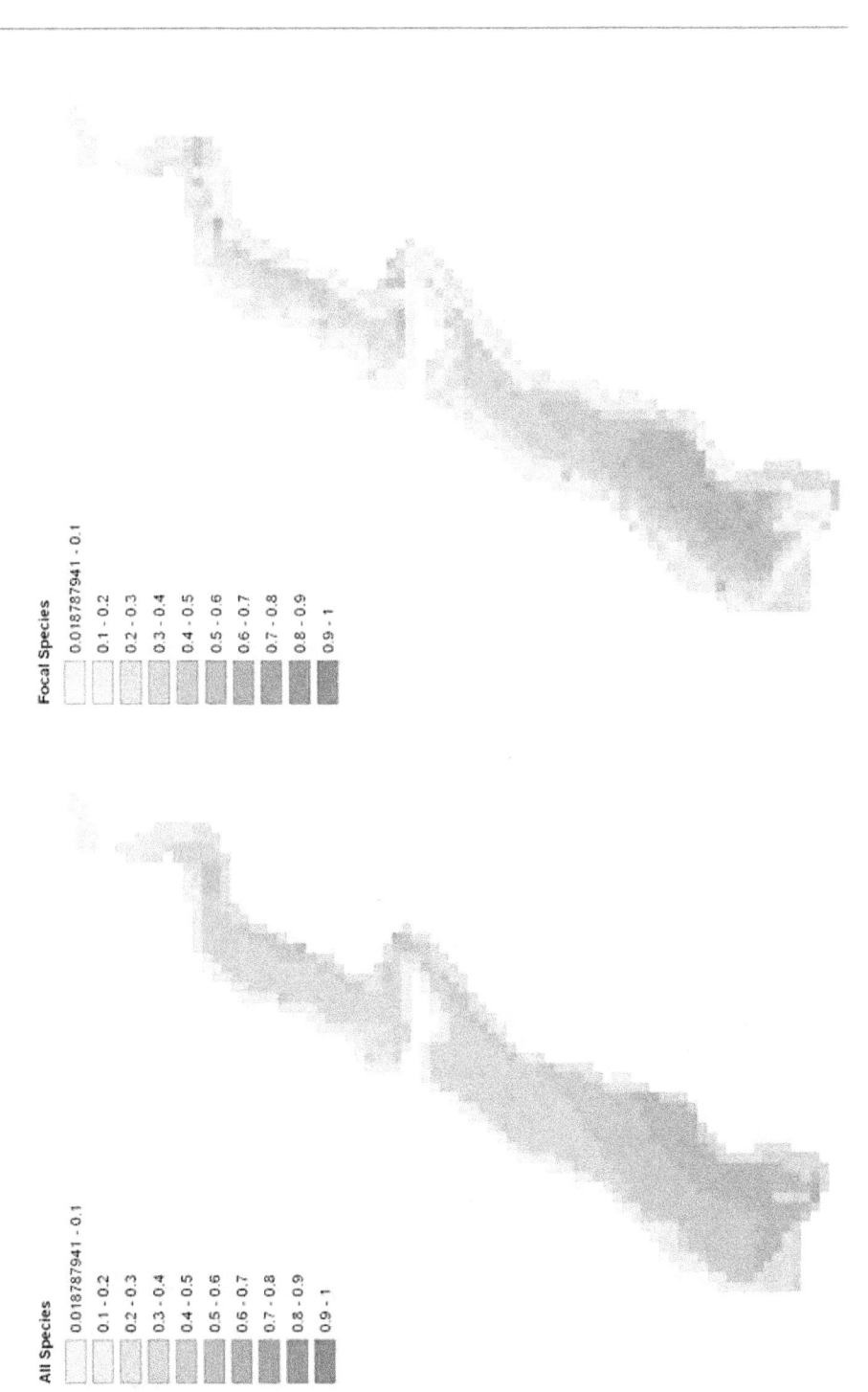

Figure 27. Probability of invasive plant establishment in areas of the de-watered Lake Aldwell reservoir determined using logistic regression equations based on observations collected between the Glines Canyon Dam and Highway 101 for (A) all invasive species observations, and (B) focal species observations.

Figure 28. Probability of invasive plant establishment in areas of the de-watered Lake Mills reservoir determined using logistic regression equations based on observations collected between the Glines Canyon Dam and Highway 101 for (A) all invasive species observations, and (B) focal species observations.

All Species

- 0.01878787941 - 0.1
- 0.1 - 0.2
- 0.2 - 0.3
- 0.3 - 0.4
- 0.4 - 0.5
- 0.5 - 0.6
- 0.6 - 0.7
- 0.7 - 0.8
- 0.8 - 0.9
- 0.9 - 1

Focal Species

- 0.01878787941 - 0.1
- 0.1 - 0.2
- 0.2 - 0.3
- 0.3 - 0.4
- 0.4 - 0.5
- 0.5 - 0.6
- 0.6 - 0.7
- 0.7 - 0.8
- 0.8 - 0.9
- 0.9 - 1

Figure 29. Predicted areas between Glines Canyon Dam and Highway 101 vulnerable to invasive plants using logistic regression equations based on observations collected in this area for (A) all invasive species observations, and (B) focal species observations compared with those observations.

Table 1. Invasive species surveyed in the Elwha River valley, Olympic National Park, Washington. [Washington State Noxious Weed Control Board classification: A=Non-native species that have limited distribution and State law requires that they be eradicated; B=Non-native species that are either absent from or limited in distribution in some parts of the State but very abundant in other areas. Management goals are to contain the plants where they are already abundant and prevent their spread to new areas; C=Non-native plants that are already widespread in Washington State. Counties can choose to enforce control, or they can educate residents about control]

Scientific name	Family	Common name	Survey 2001	High concern	Focal	WA class	Records
Arctium minus Bernh.	Asteraceae	Common burdock	X				136
Bromus tectorum L.	Poaceae	Cheatgrass					1
Buddleja davidii Franch.	Buddlejaceae	Butterfly bush		X		B	1
Calystegia sepium (L.) R. Br.ssp. *sepium*	Convolulaceae	Wild morning glory	X				4
Centaurea jacea L.	Asteraceae	Brown knapweed	X			B	24
Cirsium arvense (L.) Scop.	Asteraceae	Canada thistle	X	X	X	C	257
Cirsium vulgare (Savi) Ten.	Asteraceae	Bull thistle	X	X		C	361
Cytisus scoparius (L.) Link	Fabaceae	Scot's broom	X	X	X	B	78
Dactylis glomerata L.	Poaceae	Orchard grass	X				348
Digitalis purpurea	Scrophulariaceae	Purple foxglove					29
Erechtites minima (Poir.) DC.	Asteraceae	Toothed coast burnweed	X				4
Geranium robertianum L.	Geraniaceae	Herb Robert	X	X	X	B	356
Hedera helix L.	Araliaceae	English ivy	X	X			8
Hypericum perforatum L.	Clusiaceae	Common St. John's-wort	X	X	X	C	87
Ilex aquifolium L.	Aquifoliaceae	English holly	X	X			14
Lathyrus latifolius L.	Fabaceae	Everlasting peavine	X				5
Lathyrus sylvestris L.	Fabaceae	Small everlasting peavine	X	X	X		136
Phalaris arundinacea L.	Poaceae	Reed canarygrass	X	X	X	C	223
Polygonum cuspidatum Siebold & Zucc.	Polygonaceae	Japanese knotweed	X	X		B	10
Polygonum sachalinense F. Schmidt ex Maxim.	Polygonaceae	Giant knotweed	X	X		B	2
Polygonum x bohemicum (J. Chrtek & Chrtkovβ) Zika & Jacobson [cuspidatum x sachalinense]	Polygonaceae	Bohemian knotweed				B	1
Potentilla recta L.	Rosaceae	Sulfur cinquefoil	X			B	5
Prunus laurocerasus L.	Rosaceae	Laurel cherry	X				1
Rubus armeniacus Focke	Rosaceae	Himalayan blackberry	X	X	X	C	43
Rubus laciniatus Willd.	Rosaceae	Evergreen blackberry	X	X	X	C	6
Rumex crispus L.	Polygonaceae	Curly dock	X				53
Senecio jacobaea L.	Asteraceae	Tansy ragwort	X				17
Vicia hirsute (L.) Gray	Fabaceae	Hairy vetch	X			B	40
Vicia sativa L. ssp. *sativa*	Fabaceae	Common vetch	X				46
Vicia villosa Roth	Fabaceae	Wooly vetch	X				1

Table 2. Total number of observations, number of 50×50 m grid cells containing focal species, and percentage of grid cells by subarea with species present, Elwha River, Olympic National Park, Washington.

Focal species	Abbreviation	Total records	Total grid cells	Total grid cells (% with species)	Subareas (percentage of grid cells with species)						
					Lake Aldwell	Lake Aldwell Delta	Glines Canyon Dam to U.S. Highway 101, Wolf Creek Trail	Lake Mills	Lake Mills Delta	Geyser Valley	Hot Springs Road
Cirsium arvense	CirArv	257	232	21.2	3.1	1.4	4.0	0.5	17.8	13.6	1.4
Cytisus scoparius	CytSco	78	75	6.8	1.3	3.7	3.5	0.5	0	0	3.2
Geranium robertianum	GerRob	356	324	29.6	0.4	26.4	15.9	0	1.5	1.9	6.8
Hypericum perforatum	HypPer	87	81	7.4	1.8	9.9	2.2	0.4	2.0	1.4	0.5
Lathyrus sylvestris	LatSyl	136	128	11.7	0.4	5.8	7.7	0	0	0	0.5
Phalaris arundinacea	PhaAru	223	214	19.5	5.7	35.1	6.9	0.4	0.5	0.1	0
Rubus spp.	RubSpp	49	42	3.8	0.9	6.6	1.4	0.4	0	0	0
Total		1,186	1,096	100	13.6	88.9	41.6	2.2	21.8	17.0	12.4

Table 3. Maximum likelihood odds ratios for predictor variables and cross-validation results for logistic regression models predicting the occurrence of invasive species in sites across the entire study area and by subarea, Elwha River, Olympic National Park, Washington.

[Locations of subareas are shown in figure 2. Species: Abbreviations of species are defined in table 2. Odds ratios less than 1 indicate that the variable decreases the probability of species occurrence; odds ratios greater than 1 indicate that the variable increases the probability of species occurrence. Only statistically significant variables (α≤0.05) are presented. Elev., elevation; No. Obs., number of observations; Ppt., precipitation; SR-Jul, solar radiation on July 22]

Species	Location	n	Proximity to vector[1] — Water	Road	Trail	Environmental variables: Elev.	Precip	Slope	SR-Jul	Bare	Herbs	Low shrubs	Tall shrubs	Low trees	Tall trees	Percent correctly predicted
CirArv	All	232	0.996							0.987	1.028	1.040		1.055		93.6[2]
	Geyser Valley	85		1.001		0.931				0.963					0.988	86.4
	Mills Delta	35				0.743	1.094				1.030			1.046		79.1
	Glines-101	58		0.996								1.037				95.9
	Aldwell Delta	33				0.922								1.043		85.6
CytSco	All	75		0.997			0.984					1.035		1.048		97.9
	Glines-101	50	0.985	0.995										1.037		96.5
GerRob	All	328	0.995				0.831	0.948		0.968				1.032		90.9
	Glines-101	228	0.996	0.998		0.968	1.046				0.985			1.027		84.0
	Aldwell Delta	64		1.002									1.177			76.5
HypPer	All	81				0.987					1.025	1.057		1.067		97.7
	Glines-101	33		0.996						1.030	1.091			1.071		97.6[3]
	Aldwell Delta	24												1.070		90.1
LatSyl	All	128	0.988	0.997	0.999		0.954					1.037		1.053		96.3
	Glines-101	111	0.989	0.997		0.989										92.0
PhaAru	All	214	0.989			0.971				0.985		1.027		1.035		94.1[2]
	Glines-101	99	0.989			0.953										93.0
	Aldwell Delta	85				0.855				0.973	0.957					71.2[2]
	Lake Aldwell	26	0.975				1.220							1.062		94.2[2]
RubSpp	All	42		0.978		0.974						1.043		1.052		98.9
	Glines-101	20		0.991	0.997	0.939		1.070								98.6[3]
All	Glines-101	343		0.998		0.984					1.009	1.020		1.033		73.5
All Focal	Glines-101	298		0.998		0.976	1.011	1.037	1.001			1.027		1.035		77.4

[1] Odds ratios <1 for proximity vectors indicate higher probability of species occurrence near to vector.

[2] P-value for chi-squared is less than 0.05, indicating poor relationship.

[3] Model has more than one variable per 10 observations.

Table 4. Falling velocities of focal species, other species of concern and related species reported by Tackenberg (2001).

[m/s, meters per second]

Species	Falling velocity (m/s)
Cirsium arvense	0.2– 0.4
Centaurea jacea	3.4– 4.1
Geranium pratense	3.7
Geranium sylvaticum	2.8–3.0
Hieraciuim aurantiacum	0.3
Hypericum perforatum	1.3
Hypochaerus radicata	0.3– 0.4
Lathyrus pratensis	3.0
Potentilla erecta	1.7– 2.3
Prunus spinosa	5.5
Senecio jacobea	0.4 – 1.0

Table 5. Summary of wind speed and direction detected at Hurricane Ridge RAWS station for July 15–September 30, 1999–2008, Olympic National Park, Washington.

[Values indicate percentage of time wind came from each direction (average values greater than 3 percent are in bold). %, percent; m/s, meters per second]

Year	N	NNE	NE	ENE	E	ESE	SE	SSE	S	SSW	SW	WSW	W	WNW	NW	NNW	Calm
1999	11.0	0.8	1.4	2.5	2.1	1.3	6.9	7.0	3.2	1.3	1.0	0.8	3.1	1.7	0.8	4.2	50.9
2000	8.2	6.9	1.0	0.5	2.1	1.7	0.8	0.9	12.0	10.3	1.8	1.2	1.0	0.9	1.0	1.2	45.3
2001	8.9	6.4	2.8	2.8	4.2	3.0	3.4	3.0	3.3	3.0	2.1	2.4	2.1	2.5	2.6	4.2	43.2
2002	7.3	13.8	1.8	0.8	2.5	2.0	1.1	1.9	8.8	4.4	0.9	0.9	1.1	0.8	1.1	4.6	46.2
2003	4.6	5.8	0.6	0.5	1.7	3.7	1.1	1.8	14.0	6.1	1.4	0.6	0.6	0.3	0.8	2.1	54.3
2004	3.2	6.0	0.5	0.7	1.8	3.1	1.4	1.7	18.0	11.2	1.9	0.4	0.2	0.8	1.3	2.3	45.8
2005	0.4	6.7	3.3	1.2	7.8	2.6	0.5	0.4	0	0	0	0.1	0	0	0	0	77.0
2006	0.3	1.9	1.7	1.0	5.1	0.3	0.4	0.1	0	0	0	0	0	0	0	0	89.1
2007	0.1	0.9	1.9	1.2	18.0	0.3	0.5	0.3	0	0	0	0	0	0	0	0	76.6
2008	7.2	1.3	0.7	0.8	2.9	1.3	1.6	16.1	16.0	1.6	1.0	1.6	0.9	0.6	1.7	2.1	42.8
Avg %	5.1	5.0	1.6	1.2	4.8	1.9	1.8	3.3	7.5	3.8	1.0	0.8	0.9	0.8	0.9	2.1	57.1
Max (m/s)	12-15	9-12	9-12	9-12	9-12	9-12	9-12	9-12	15-18	9-12	6-9	9-12	9-12	9-12	12-15	9-12	<1.3

Table 6. Comparison of wind speed and direction predicted by WindNinja with actual conditions at Glines Canyon Dam, Elwha River, Olympic National Park, Washington.

[m/s, meters per second; Dir, direction; °, degrees]

	Hurricane Ridge conditions					
	From North, 15 m/s n = 5		From east, 12 m/s n = 5		From south, 18 m/s n = 7	
	Dir (°)	Speed (m/s)	Dir (°)	Speed (m/s)	Dir (o)	Speed (m/s)
WindNinja prediction	15-19	19-21	316-324	5-6	195-200	23-25
Glines Canyon Dam (average)	166	6	302	7	203	16
Glines Canyon Dam (range)	92-194	0-12	217-26	4-9	173-233	3-26

Table 7. Potential destinations of *Cirsium arvense* seeds from present populations as a result of wind dispersal from the most common wind patterns based on output from the WindNinja model, Elwha River, Washington.

	Wind Direction (Source)		
Current Location	North	East	South
Geyser Valley	Up valley on western side of river	Down valley, possibly terrace SW of Rica Canyon	Downstream to Lake Mills Reservoir
Lake Mills delta	Terrace southwest of Rica Canyon	Eastern shore Lake Mills	Downstream to Lake Mills Reservoir
Lake Aldwell delta	Herrick road area, river valley to south	Plateau northwest of U.S. Highway101–Elwha River intersection	Southern Lake Aldwell delta and upland area to west

Table 8. High priority potential sources of exotic species as a result of wind dispersal from the most common wind patterns based on output from the WindNinja model, Elwha River, Washington.

	Wind Direction (Source)		
Reservoir	North	East	South
Lake Aldwell	–All areas due north including Elwha River delta	None	–Hillslope east of Lake Aldwell
Lake Mills	–Elwha River valley bottom to north –Herrick Road plateau –Hillslope west of Glines Canyon Dam	None	–Plateau southwest of Lake Mills

Table 9. Summary of species traits for focal species and species of high concern that can be used to prioritize species threat, and the resulting priority.

[Species data are from Washington State (2009). Habitat: Habitat with which species has been associated. Characteristics indicating a high priority for removal are indicated in bold. NA, not applicable; yr, year; veg, vegetation]

Species	Vectors	Time to flower	Habitat	Removal difficulty	Spread rate	Priority
Buddleja spp.	Wind **Water**	**First yr**	**River banks**	**High** – seed bank	**Rapid**	**High**
Cirsium arvense	**Water** Wind	**NA** (veg spread)	**Waterways**	**High**- herbicides	**Rapid**	**High**
Cytisus scoparius	**Water**	> 3 yrs	**River banks**	**High** – seed bank	Moderate	Mid
Geranium robertianum	Elk Machinery	**First yr**	Forests, meadows	Moderate	**Rapid**	Mid
Hedera helix	Birds	10 yrs	Forests	Easy	**Rapid**	Low
Hypericum perforatum	Elk	First yr or 2 to several yrs	**Bare**	**High**	?	Mid
Ilex aquifolium	Birds	2–10 yrs	Forests	Moderate	Slow	Low
Lathyrus sylvestris	**Water**	**First yr**	Disturbance	?	Moderate	Mid
Phalaris arundinacea	**Water**	**First yr**	**River banks**	**High**	**Rapid**	**High**
Polygonum spp.	**Water** Wind	**NA** (veg spread)	**Flood zone**	**High**	**Rapid**	**High**
Rubus spp.	Birds	2^+ yrs	**River flats**	**High**	**Rapid**	Mid

Table 10. Summary of areas, species of concern that are already present (searched areas), or potentially present (areas not searched), and potential management actions, Elwha River, Washington.

[Priority vectors and species are indicated in bold. Abbreviations of species of concern are defined in table 2]

History	Area	Vectors	Species of concern	Management action
Not searched; outside of Park	North of Lake Aldwell	Wind	**CirArv** BudSpp	Advocate mowing
	Herrick Road	Wind Elk Birds	**CirArv** LatSyl **PhaAru**	
Searched	Aldwell Delta	Wind **Water**	**CirArv** GerRob LatSyl **PhaAru**	Options: Remove entire plants Remove flowers or seeds
	Lake Aldwell to northern end of Lake Mills	Wind **Water** Birds	**CirArv** CytSco GerRob HedHel HypPer IleAqu LatSyl **PhaAru** RubSpp	
	Lake Mills Delta	Wind **Water** Elk	**CirArv** GerRob HypPer **PhaAru**	
	Geyser Valley	**Water** Elk	**CirArv** GerRob HypPer **PhaAru**	
	Glines Canyon Dam	**Machinery**	CytSco GerRob HypPer	
	Elwha Dam	**Machinery**	**CirArv** CytSco GerRob HypPer LatSpp **PhaAru** **PolSpp** RubSpp	
Not searched; inside of Park	Between roads, western side of Lake Mills	Birds	CytSco GerRob HedHel HypPer IleAqu RubSpp	Search and remove
	Western side Lake Mills, southern end, plateau and drainages	Wind **Water** Elk	**CirArv** GerRob HypPer LatSyl **PhaAru** **PolSpp** RubSpp	

www.ingramcontent.com/pod-product-compliance
Lightning Source LLC
Chambersburg PA
CBHW080435290526
45791CB00008BA/2510